To Nolie & Beka,

[signature]

6/16/21

Nampa, ID

THAT REMINDS ME OF A STORY

A Collection of Stories
Sharing the Business
Wisdom of the
Zamzow Family

Art Gregory and Jim Zamzow

That Reminds Me of a Story
A Collection of Stories Sharing the Business Wisdom of the Zamzow Family
By Art Gregory
Jim Zamzow © 2021

Zamzows Inc. supports copyright. Copyright fuels creativity, encourages diverse voices, promotes free speech, and creates a vibrant culture. Thank you for buying an authorized edition of this book and for complying with copyright laws by not reproducing, scanning, or distributing any part of it in any form without permission. You are supporting authors and allowing publishers to continue to publish books for every reader.

While the publisher and author have used their best efforts in preparing this book, they make no representations or warranties with respect to the accuracy or completeness of this book and specifically disclaim any implied warranties of merchantability or fitness for a particular purpose. No warranty may be created or extended by sales representatives or written sales materials. The stories and interviews in this book are true although the exact details may be remembered by others slightly differently.

The publisher and author shall have neither liability nor responsibility to any person or entity with respect to loss, damage, or injury caused or alleged to be caused directly or indirectly by the information contained in this book. The information presented herein is in no way intended as a substitute for counseling or other professional guidance.

Cover and Interior Design: Fusion Creative Works, FusionCW.com
Lead Editor: Megan Terry
Book production by Aloha Publishing

ISBN: 978-1-61206-236-5

Printed in Canada

For my children and grandchildren, that they might get a sense of how our family evolved. Be true to yourselves and beware of manipulators.

—Jim Zamzow

Contents

Foreword	9
Introduction	11
Zamzow Family Tree	15
Introducing the Zamzow Family	17
The History of the Family Business	31
Zamzows 10 Business Commandments	
1: Honesty Goes Both Ways	39
2: Defend Yourself and What You Love	51
3: Hard Work, High Standards, No Shortcuts	61
4: Going Beyond Expectations	71
5: Finding New Products and Ideas	81
6: If You Want to Do It Right, Make It Yourself	93
7: Bigger Is Not Always Better	103
8: There's Nothing Like Money in the Bank	109
9: Employees Make Your Business	119
10: A Good Steward to the Community Earth	127
Conclusion	149
Zamzows Now	151
Acknowledgments	155
About the Authors	157

Foreword

By Jim Zamzow

Stories have been the method of information transfer since before written language. In my family, stories were told by both sets of my grandparents and parents. They were always both educational and entertaining. In fact, I thought most of the stories were more just to entertain us kids, until later years when I discovered them to be true. I passed on as many stories to my children as I could recall and as they grew a little older, I was accused of repeating them way too often. After I finished college and went to work for my family business, I had many experiences that were fun for me to tell.

When Art Gregory joined our company as communications and marketing director, we built an in-house recording studio. Art would write the ads and I would record them as the company voice. What should have taken about 20 minutes to complete a 60-second radio ad often took two hours because of our conversations, which most times included a story I would tell Art. I didn't know it at the time, but Art was recording the stories and often including them in radio ads. Years later, when Art decided to further his education and earn a master's degree in communications, he compiled stories as told by myself and other members of my family as part of his master's thesis and thus this book.

Great families are held together over generations by the family mores, a combination of moral, ethical, spiritual, and business ideas. The mores are then taught by the elders to the children as they grow and develop. Sometimes these points are punctuated by discipline and in my case emotional and physical punishment. I think for my personality I needed a little of both.

THAT REMINDS ME OF A STORY

My intent in publishing this book is to pass on to my future generations of grandchildren some stories that may be forgotten with my passing. I want them to know the history of the Zamzow family and know their grandparents, and I hope that they take the messages of these stories to heart. At the same time, I'd like to help others who weren't blessed with a family to teach them. Each story carries something that anyone can learn from. We use stories to teach lessons about life and business. My hope is that reading this will help you make better business decisions.

The soul of these stories is compassion. Even though the stories sometimes show some members of the family doing things we shouldn't have done, those are lessons we can also learn from. I have been blessed in so many ways, and since I'm not the sharpest crayon in the box, I have had to learn many lessons by experience through the school of hard knocks.

I am so grateful to all of my family, both current and past, for the lessons they have taught me, and to all of my many mentors who appeared when I needed them most. One of those mentors was my dear friend Kirby Buchanan, who used to tell me, "God chastens those He loves." And that reminds me of a story . . .

—*Jim Zamzow*

Introduction

Zamzows Inc. was founded by August and Carmalita Zamzow in 1933. The company grew from one small store in Boise to many stores across the greater Treasure Valley. Four generations of the Zamzow family have owned and managed the company. The underlying business philosophy and culture of the company has remained the same, consistently passed down from generation to generation. It's summed up in what they call the Zamzows Way: "To provide the highest quality, environmentally-sound products at a service level beyond our customers' expectations."

Zamzows is remarkable as a family-owned business and as a piece of Idaho history. As a company, Zamzows has made a difference in the lives of Idaho residents and set an example for other businesses in the valley. The Zamzow family derives pleasure from serving other people's needs, and the education and awareness the Zamzows company creates has an even larger impact than the products they sell.

Many family-owned businesses face statistically poor survival rates past the first generation of owners. Yet Zamzows has made it to its fourth generation and is more successful than ever. By learning how and why Zamzows has become the success it is today, other businesses and entrepreneurs can learn from the Zamzows model and employ its beneficial practices.

This book began as part of my master's thesis project in 2003. As a Zamzows Inc. employee, I knew that the owners of the company, Jim and Rick Zamzow, told certain stories over and over. These stories are a valuable way Zamzows defines its organizational culture, so I decided to collect them.

THAT REMINDS ME OF A STORY

After interviewing Zamzow family members, some distinct themes and lessons emerged in the stories they told. While each of the 64 stories had at least one central theme, some stories incorporated multiple themes or lessons. I then converted these themes into:

Zamzows Ten Commandments of Good Business

1. Be honest in all matters. The customer is entitled to full value for his or her dollar.
2. Be prepared to defend yourself and what you love. You never know what will happen.
3. Work hard and have quality standards in all you do. Learn from others but build your own customer base, one customer at a time, whatever way you can.
4. Always do what's best for the customer. Go beyond his or her expectations.
5. Be innovative. Search out and develop new ideas and products, and then have the courage to stick with them.
6. Develop your own *superior* brands so you can control the quality and protect your market.
7. Grow your business only as fast as you can handle it. Bigger is not always better.
8. Avoid borrowing money; if you have to, pay it back quickly.
9. Employees make your company; seek out and hire good ones, train them, learn from them, and then do what's necessary to retain them.
10. Be a good steward of the earth's resources and all living things on it. We're all part of one big community.

INTRODUCTION

These overriding themes reveal some basic survival skills for small family businesses. I grouped these stories by theme in order to identify the point the storyteller was trying to make.

The stories told by the Zamzow family—including Carmalita, Bernie, Jim, and Rick—have helped shape the basic business philosophy and practices of the Zamzows company and its employees. The stories convey a unique culture that embraces the values of the family.

The stories are told for a reason, though what that reason is varies with the needs of the storyteller. Members of the Zamzow family often say in conversation, "And that reminds me of a story." Each story is brought up in response to a situation or topic, whatever "that" refers to, and often for the purpose of sharing the value or point the story illustrates.

The morals found in the stories are inviting, fun, and inspiring. While company policies could be stated in cold, corporate language in an employee handbook, a story makes a more memorable and fun way to teach employees, and employees are more likely to take it to heart. The stories illustrate why a rule should be followed and what can happen if it isn't taken seriously.

The Zamzow family passes stories down to family members from generation to generation, and then tells them to their employees. While stories circulate within every family-owned business, it's not often that they survive through several generations of business operations.

Zamzows Inc., now in its fourth generation as a family-owned company, has survived while most family-owned businesses have failed. Zamzows has *what it takes*. According to Jim Collins, author of the bestseller *Built to Last*, what it takes are five qualities family-owned companies must have to survive.

1. A core purpose describing what you stand for and why you exist.
2. The desire to create an enduring company, not just an easy place for family members to work.
3. A set of values and ideas that is deeply held and followed with dedication.
4. A family that shares the core values with everyone in the company.
5. A guiding principle that is more important than just making money.

THAT REMINDS ME OF A STORY

Zamzows Inc. has all five of Collins' *Built to Last* qualities. Telling stories plays an important role in keeping a community intact and moving toward a common goal.

Through the telling of stories, Zamzows employees understand and embrace core organizational values and a core purpose. They have created and sustained the culture and community of Zamzows Inc. This community embraces common beliefs and values, and a shared vision, through sharing these stories with each other.

The stories in this book are much more than just narratives. They serve specific contextual purposes and are told to strategically illuminate a specific culture-bearing message. They also help establish and enforce codes of employee conduct and ethics.

Beyond the organization, there is plenty we can learn from these stories. The Zamzow family and Zamzows Inc. are both important parts of Idaho history. They've had a major impact on the community and their stories are important to remember in their role in shaping Idaho.

The company is significant because of how it has made a difference in people's lives—the animals they feed, the gardens and lawns they treat, and the amount of chemical fertilizer Jim has kept out of the soil by developing and promoting nonchemical fertilizers.

Zamzows has had an impact on the community of the Treasure Valley and beyond. In addition to the products they've developed, they've contributed greatly to charity efforts and to creating a cleaner environment. But perhaps the most profound impact they've had is the education and awareness the business spreads through their radio advertisements and through their service to their customers, providing excellent value and quality and teaching others to take care of the earth.

Since 1933, it has remained family owned and has held onto the same values and core principles since the beginning. And the Zamzow family is freely willing to share what has made them successful to help make others successful.

Zamzow Family Tree

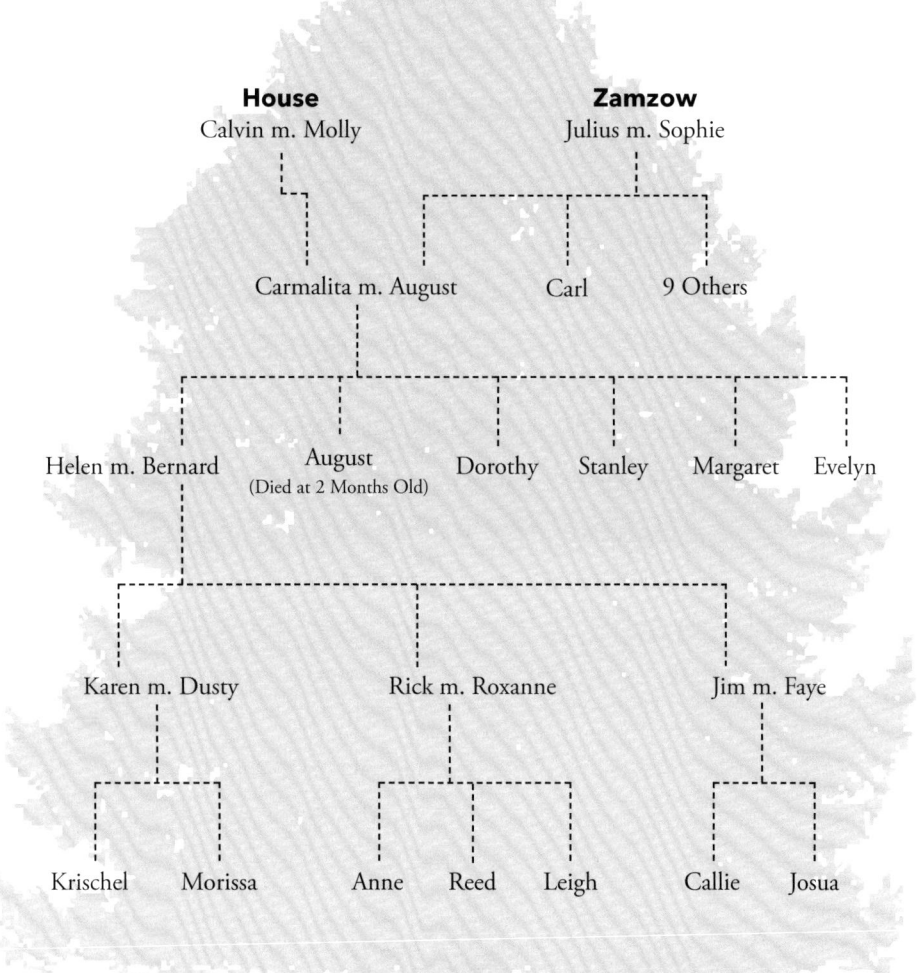

House
Calvin m. Molly

Zamzow
Julius m. Sophie

Carmalita m. August — Carl — 9 Others

Helen m. Bernard — August (Died at 2 Months Old) — Dorothy — Stanley — Margaret — Evelyn

Karen m. Dusty — Rick m. Roxanne — Jim m. Faye

Krischel — Morissa — Anne — Reed — Leigh — Callie — Josua

Introducing the Zamzow Family

It Started With Grandma Z

The Zamzows legend began with Carmalita, born to Mr. and Mrs. Calvin Lee House on March 19, 1897, in rural Knox County, Missouri. Her mother named her Carmalita after a character in a book she was reading. Perhaps reading that book had taken her mind off the four years of drought her family had endured. When relatives returned from Idaho with tales of booming fortunes in the town of Boise, Carmalita's dad said, "That's it." He held an auction and sold the farm. The House family was moving.

But it would be hard to leave Missouri. A few years ago the House family hadn't even heard of Idaho. They planned to travel by train, and Mr. House would have to find a job and work to save enough money to buy a farm.

Just nine days shy of her fifth birthday on the day they left, little Carmalita was in for a long ride and a great adventure. It took five days to reach Idaho. The family was hopeful about the rich farmland and jobs available in Idaho so

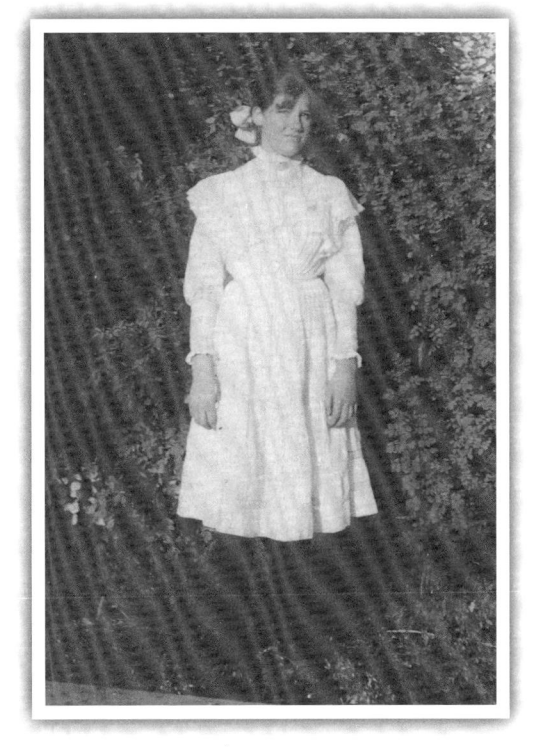

Carmalita House, 1911

THAT REMINDS ME OF A STORY

Carmalita's father could support the family in the way they deserved. After four straight years of drought in Missouri, Carmalita had never lived with enough water until they reached Idaho, which seemed like a promised land to them.

Mr. and Mrs. House, 5-year-old Carmalita, and her 3-year-old brother Merle had traveled over 1,500 miles in a hot railway car, known as an "immigrant car" because everything the family owned, including a live cow, traveled together. Whenever the train stopped, the cow was let out to eat and drink.

The train arrived in Meridian on March 10, 1902. At the time, Meridian had a railway station while Boise did not. That meant the family had to travel to Boise by wagon. They camped that night at what is now the Western Idaho Fairgrounds.

For the next two weeks, the family secured room and board at the Overland Hotel in downtown Boise. Calvin found employment immediately with J.M. Neil Transfer, a local moving company, and the family rented an apartment in Boise's Hyde Park on 13th Street.

Calvin House didn't like working for someone else, but a steady paycheck was what the family needed. They saved their money and bought four lots in Boise's north end. Calvin built a small house on one of the lots and the family lived in Boise for almost four years while the land appreciated. When Calvin finally sold the house and the other three lots, he was able to purchase an 80-acre farm on the corner of Ustick and Locust Grove in Meridian.

The House family grew and Carmalita eventually had eight brothers and sisters. There would have been 10 in all but her mother had lost a baby girl right after Carmalita. Her brothers were Merle, Anthony, Edgar, Olen, and Cletus, also known as "Doc." Her sisters were Kathryn, Irene, and Laverne. It was well known that when someone asked, "Is there a House in the house?" the answer would be "Which one do you want? We have a house full of Houses!"

During Carmalita's childhood in Meridian, there were no paved roads in the whole town. And worse yet, no road graders. She recalled, "I don't think they knew what a road grader was at that time because the roads were nothing but mud." To avoid muddy shoes on the way to school, Carmalita and her brothers and sisters "walked the fences" along the rural roads that led to the schoolhouse.

INTRODUCING THE ZAMZOW FAMILY

"I don't think the farmers liked us too much," she said, "because we'd stand on the barbed-wire fences and walk sideways down the fence to keep our shoes out of the mud. Eventually all the fence wires began to sag."

When there wasn't mud on the roads due to water or snow, there was dust in the summer. "My mother used to take a jug of water and a towel in the wagon when we'd go to town because the horses would kick up so much dust." The family took the wagon to Boise once a week to attend Mass at St. John's Catholic Church, and their mother would clean them all up after the ride before they went into church.

As the oldest child, Carmalita had to drop out of high school to help support the family. But she didn't think anything about it. She'd been taught to do the right thing, even if it meant personal sacrifice. She later married August Zamzow, and in 1933, she helped found Zamzows Inc.

Carmalita came to be known as "Grandma Z" to dozens of grandchildren, great-grandchildren, and great-great-grandchildren. She lived to be 104. She almost never became ill and attributed her health to the way she ate. She always had a beautiful garden and made good use of organic matter long before composting became popular.

Grandma Z Says . . .

I never had a garbage hauler. Anything that was food or plant I put back into the soil. I figured that's where it came from in the first place and the soil needed it. I also buried my tin cans in the soil. I figured the soil needed the extra iron.

Grandma Z's most precious possessions were not material things—her family was most dear to her, along with what it stood for. Carmalita died on October 13, 2001. She lived a full and wonderful life, and, when she left us, she was ready to be with the Lord. Carmalita Zamzow taught her family a great deal, lessons about life and about business. The values she passed on are reflected in the Zamzows' company culture and in the stories in this book.

The Town and the Family Named Zamzow

Not much is known about the origin of the name Zamzow, which, according to Grandma Z, was properly pronounced Zam-zoe, to rhyme with "grow." Many people mispronounce it Zam-zouw, to rhyme with "cow." Carmalita's son Bernie explained, "It goes either way. We prefer Zam-zoe. There are a lot of Zamzows in the United States and I've run across several in my travels. Some of them went by Zam-zoe and some went with Zam-zouw. It's immaterial. We answer to both."

But efforts to discover the origin of the Zamzow name and how they got to America from Germany have proven tricky. Carmalita asked her in-laws how the family came to America.

Bernie said, "I never could get very much information about our family from my dad. I guess he was a typical German—quiet-mouthed—or just didn't care to talk about it."

Bernie speculated there may have been an escape from East Germany (or Prussia, as it was then known). "They may have been afraid to tell anyone for fear something might happen to them, or perhaps to someone left behind." When Bernie joined the U.S. Army in World War II, he discovered there was a town called Zamzow in Germany.

He ran across a young Zamzow who lived in Bellingham, Washington, and the man said, "Did you know where the Zamzows originated?"

Bernie replied, "Well, no, but I've heard stories. I even asked my dad if our name might have been Zamzowski or some other variation."

The man said, "Oh no, there's a community in East Germany that was named Zamzow. I have a map that shows it! Would you like a copy?"

He gave Bernie a copy of an old map and told him the folks named Zamzow who farmed the land lived on the higher ground but grew their crops on the lowlands. The name of the town was Zamzow.

Not much is known about Zamzow, Germany, beyond the map Bernie picked up while in the Army. Jim Zamzow ran into a man who seemed to know all about it.

INTRODUCING THE ZAMZOW FAMILY

His name was Dakow. Jim asked him how he knew how to pronounce their name, and he said he knew about the Zamzow name and where it came from because his name came from the same area. The "kow" in his name was pronounced "koe." Both names were Prussian.

Genealogical searches of the name Zamzow yield a host of individuals born in Posen, Prussia. Zamzows Inc.'s co-founder, August Lewis Zamzow, was the only one of his three brothers born in the United States. It is highly possible that the family hailed from Zamzow, Prussia, immigrated to the U.S., and settled in the upper Midwest, as did many other German immigrants at the time.

The Oregon shortline railroad. August and Carl rode a train similar to this one. (Courtesy Idaho State Archives)

How the Zamzow Name Got to Idaho

August Lewis Zamzow was born January 6, 1894, in Hayfield, Minnesota. He was raised strictly by his German Lutheran parents. When he was just 19 years old, he and his brother Carl embarked on an adventure that would change their lives forever.

THAT REMINDS ME OF A STORY

Carmalita and August Zamzow

Carmalita and August with granddaughter Karen

Bernie Zamzow

INTRODUCING THE ZAMZOW FAMILY

As young men, August and Carl wanted to leave home and work for themselves. They'd both worked in Minnesota and the Dakotas. Their older brother had already gone west and was living in California. He told them how great it was and they decided they'd go to California as well.

So they stowed away on a train—they called it "riding the rails"—and got all the way to Idaho. When the train stopped at the station in Meridian, they were hungry and August said, "I'll run downtown and get us a sandwich."

It was about a half mile to the store and August made it back just as the train started to pull out. He ran as fast as he could but couldn't get back onboard! Carl tried to pull him onto the train, but he couldn't make it, and August was left stranded in Meridian. Fortunately, being an aggressive sort of a guy, it didn't take him long to find work and lodging.

August Zamzow Starts a Family

No one knows where August Zamzow first lived after arriving in Meridian. Carmalita said he worked for a farmer who brought August into the bakery where she was working and that's how they met. However, Carmalita's oldest son, Bernie, said his dad worked for Calvin House, Carmalita's dad.

Regardless of who August worked for, the visits to Beam's Bakery were the start of their romance. August and Carmalita were married in the parish house behind St. John's Catholic Church in Boise on February 10, 1915. Because August was German Lutheran, not Catholic, they couldn't get married in the church itself.

Bernie Zamzow was born in April 1916 in Star, Idaho, in a little red house. August and Carmalita had five kids. Bernie describes Carmalita as a hard worker and a good mother.

During Bernie's early childhood, the family grew and moved frequently as August worked for different farmers. They eventually rented a farm on Chinden Boulevard between Locust Grove and Meridian Road, then moved north of Meridian to Ustick at the old Colonel Marster's farm. Finally, August bought a farm at Franklin and Cole.

THAT REMINDS ME OF A STORY

Some of these moves were necessitated by how the family continued to grow. But it had its share of tragedies, too. In 1918, two years after Bernie was born, Carmalita lost a child, August Vincent, to the flu. The deadly influenza epidemic of the time killed many people worldwide, including thousands of soldiers during World War I. Carmalita and August were both stricken and Carmalita developed pneumonia. She was given last rites and not expected to survive. But she recovered and went on to have four more healthy children.

There were surprisingly large age gaps between the children. Bernie was four years older than Dorothy, and Stanley came along another four years after that. Two years later, Margaret arrived, then Evelyn after another two years. That made Bernie 12 years older than Evelyn.

Bernie teased his younger siblings. He said, "I probably got more switches and belt hammerings because I was the oldest and biggest tease! I'd tease my younger brother and sisters to the point my dad or mom couldn't stand it any longer and would have to shut me up."

In addition to being a tease, Bernie Zamzow was a worker. He helped his father and mother on the farm from a young age and never stopped trying to improve himself. He got good grades in the schools he attended, including the old Maple Grove School atop the hill at Maple Grove and Franklin. At Boise High, he won a scholarship to the University of Idaho where he would meet Helen, his future wife. During the summer and after school, he helped his father on the farm, and later in the family business. Bernie eventually served in World War II and started a family. His children were Karen, Jim, and Rick.

Bernie was a stout individual. Jim recalls a big guy named Bill Boston who used to come into the Meridian Mill and regularly try to "rough up" Bernie. He explained, "This guy used to shove Pop around and grab him and try to wrestle him down. One time Pop reached up and got him in the 'Zamzow headlock.' Pop taught us how to do it when we were little kids. He just reached up from behind and powered him down!"

Rick speculated that Bernie developed such strength from throwing around 100-pound bags of feed.

INTRODUCING THE ZAMZOW FAMILY

Stanley Zamzow

Stanley Zamzow was a wiry little redhead with a personality to match. He was known to Jim and Rick as "Uncle Red," but to his mom, Carmalita, Stanley was her special little helper. She said, "Stanley would always rush home from school. It was hard for him. He never got to take part in any school activities at all. No football or baseball, which he loved. He always had to come home and help. He was my right-hand man!"

There are several legendary stories about Stanley. Carmalita's favorite story was when Stanley got in trouble with a cop.

In 1936, Carmalita's brother, Doc House, was Sheriff of Ada County. Deputy Jackson told Doc a story about stopping some "little guy" on Fairview.

Left to right: Bernie, Carmalita, August, Stanley

August was at the store and had sent Stanley down Fairview Avenue in the Ford pickup truck to get a milk can from home. Stanley was only 12 years old and so small he could barely see over the steering wheel. He got the milk can but on the way back, he ran into a cop. Stanley just headed for the store as fast as he could. The cop chased him all the way into the dirt parking lot behind the store.

Stanley pulled in just a little before the cop, but when the cop looked for the driver, there was no one in the truck. He knew the driver had to be in there, because he'd seen the truck pull in and no one got out. Searching the truck cab, he finally reached up under the dash and pulled out Stanley!

Stanley had somehow crawled underneath the big hollow dashboard and hidden up there. The cop gave him a good talking-to and Stanley just kept saying, "My dad told me to go get that milk can, so I was just doing what I was told."

The deputy told him, "After this, you tell your dad to get his own milk can!"

Stanley was well known for using nicknames. It might have started with Stanley's uncle, Cletus "Doc" House, Carmalita's youngest brother. When he was only 2 years old, Cletus would carry a tin cup of water around and whenever anyone was hurt, the little boy "doctored" them with water. Calvin House started calling him "Doc." The name stuck and he spent the rest of his life known to everyone as simply "Doc" House.

Young Stanley Zamzow may have picked up on the use of nicknames from his mother or "Uncle Doc" because to Stanley, everybody and everything had a nickname. To Stanley, manure was "zuh-murrel," possibly a corruption of the name his mother had for manure, "buh-nurrel." Stanley had names for people too. Jim was "Jimmer-Jammer" and Rick was "Ricker-Sticker." He called longtime Zamzow employee Walt Shepherd "Walter O'Toole, the Fighting Irishman," and another longtime Zamzow employee, Les Tinkham, "Holy Kadiddlehopper."

Stanley retired early from Zamzows Inc. He spent many wonderful years with his wife, Gayle, sons Doug and Barry, and daughter, Pam. Stanley passed away in February of 2002 after an injury caused by a fall on ice. Stanley Zamzow may be gone, but he'll never be forgotten. Stanley's contribution and sacrifice, both for the family and for the business, cannot be underestimated. We miss you, Uncle Red.

Jim Zamzow

When Jim was born, he was almost a toddler, according to his mother, Helen Zamzow. Jim's dad, Bernie, said, "Jim was a big boy when he was born but not a very healthy lad. He developed asthma at an early age and I remember we used to say to him, 'Now, don't run,' because whenever he'd run, he'd choke. He had a tough time as a youngster because he couldn't seem to get his lungs to open up enough to participate in sports like the other kids. Whenever he'd exert himself by running, he'd choke up. But he's pretty well overcome that now."

Jim Zamzow with pepper plant

Perhaps Jim's poor health as a child is partially behind his quest to help others. Over the years, Jim has developed countless products that improve the health of animals and humans. This may be because Jim was *raised* to serve others.

Jim's strict, German upbringing from his father was somewhat tempered by his mother Helen's more gentle nature. She was born of English and Scots-Irish heritage with some Cherokee lineage.

According to Jim, the mix of values from his two parents gave him and his brother Rick a unique perspective. "We have the discipline from our Dad's German heritage, but also have the nature, the softness, and the compassion of Native Americans in our blood. It's a pretty good blend."

Those Native American values inherited from his mother contributed to Jim's strong environmental beliefs. "That Cherokee comes out in me in a lot of ways, in an appreciation of nature and of my fellow man. I like to try to see how another person is thinking and how they're functioning, and why they're functioning the way they are. That's compassion."

Jim (left) and Rick (center) and Barry (right) at a House family picnic

Jim Zamzow has compassion for animals, compassion for people, and compassion for the earth. According to Jim, "We have a responsibility to provide products to people that will improve the quality of their lives and improve the quality of this earth."

Jim Zamzow has put his money where his mouth is. He's responsible for developing an entire line of environmentally-sound products manufactured and marketed by Zamzows. That path has not always been an easy one. Jim explains he feels a calling to do the right thing.

"I'm not doing this for the money. I'm doing it for the earth and for people. I know this is my calling. I tried years ago to quit doing this. It's frustrating to try to get people to stop, listen, and change. But most people don't want to change. I tried to quit calling on farmers, but I just can't. It's in my blood.

INTRODUCING THE ZAMZOW FAMILY

Often I wake up in the morning with a new idea that's been given to me by the grace of God. I feel I'm supposed to follow through on the idea. I'd like to think that some of the things I'm doing will help bring about a positive change, and not just in Idaho—everywhere."

Rick Zamzow

Rick's son, Reed, described his dad as strict. Both Rick and Reed love the land and being outdoors. Rick is an avid hunter and a conservationist. There's nothing he loves more than hunting behind his dogs or visiting his Payette River farm, set up as a nature preserve for wild pheasants and turkeys. But at work, Rick is all business.

Rick at Grandma Z's 99th birthday party

In fact, Reed says Rick actually fired him when Reed was working at the Federal Way store during high school. Reed left work without telling the manager, which caused some problems for the store when other employees had to pick up the slack. Rick didn't take kindly to Reed's lackadaisical attitude about his job, and when the boy returned home, Rick fired him. He later got rehired when his dad cooled down, but he never forgot that lesson. He explains, "I didn't handle myself in a professional manner. I was young at the time. I thought I could get away with it. I found out I couldn't, even if my dad owned the store."

Bernie, Rick's dad, described him as a fearless, wiry redhead. "He'd run into things and was always getting hurt because he was so reckless. He went at everything like it was the last thing he was ever going to do. When Rick was 5 or 6 years old, the older neighborhood kids would play football. Those bigger boys would run over him. But he was tough! They'd knock him down and he'd get right back up!"

Rick is still tough and fearless. But there are other sides to Rick as well. He's a highly capable administrator with a calculating, analytical side. Jim and Rick are a well-matched set of opposites; they seem to balance one another out.

Rick and Jim Zamzow as young boys

The History of the Family Business

The First Store

August Zamzow moved his family to their dream farm at the corner of Franklin and Cole in October 1928. One year later, the Great Depression began. According to Grandma Z, the family got by since they had a farm and could raise their own food, but there was no money to pay the mortgage. The farm market collapsed and farmers couldn't get a decent price for their crops. Bernie was in junior high school then and recalls those difficult times.

During the Depression, the family couldn't sell any of the produce, milk, or pigs they raised. August was discouraged and said, "If we can't make enough money to even pay the interest on our debt, there's no use staying on the farm."

August was a friend of J.M. Dodds, a banker from Meridian who later went into the real estate business. Bernie thinks it was Dodds who talked August into buying a small feed store at the corner of Fairview and Liberty in 1933. It was called the Snodgrass Mill, and they changed the name to Zamzows Coal and Feed. It was a grist mill that ground grain.

Helen and Bernie Zamzow next to gas pumps in earliest existing photo of Zamzows storefront

THAT REMINDS ME OF A STORY

The owner, Mr. Snodgrass, was likely not making his payments to the bank. Bernie speculated that was why Mr. Dodds put the deal together with August. The bank was trying to get the money they'd loaned to Mr. Snodgrass or find someone else to take on the debt.

Zamzows storefront in the early 50s before Fairview Avenue was widened

Buying the store eventually forced the Zamzows to return the family farm to the bank. This was a huge sacrifice since Carmalita never wanted to leave the farm. It was the first home they'd ever owned, and they'd established roots there. But August said, "We can't make a living on the farm and we have to find something else to do, so we'll try this."

Arthritis was also beginning to bother August Zamzow and his doctor didn't think he should be spending so much time wearing the rubber boots necessary for a lot of the farm work. He was injured on the farm, and if he didn't quit farming, it would get worse. But August traded being in irrigation boots and holding a shovel for picking up 100-pound grain sacks at the mill. It worked out in the end because they were able to keep their family afloat through the Depression.

August and Carmalita Zamzow brought their core values with them when they started Zamzows Coal and Feed in April 1933. Bernie and Stanley were schooled in these values.

Bernie said, "My parents worked hard and they expected their children to work hard too. Honesty was one of the first things we were taught. My mother was quite religious and brought us up as good Christians. My parents not only taught us their values, they lived them. Those same values naturally came into the business. In a nutshell, you have to be worthy of your customers: you must serve them, treat them properly, and be honest with them. If you don't, you won't grow. Our business has come a long way, so I'd say that the values my parents established when we were young have stayed with us."

Bernie and Stanley Take Over

The 1930s and early 1940s were lean years, not just for Zamzows Coal and Feed, but for the whole country. The nation was coming out of the Great Depression and Boise's local economy was struggling.

Bernie and Stanley helped at the store after school and during the summer. Bernie recalled how he and Stanley first got involved with the Zamzow family business. There weren't many jobs available at the time, and August was getting older. In those days, parents depended upon their children to help. Bernie was away at school most of the year and helped in the summertime. Stanley, who was in high school at the time, worked evenings and Saturdays.

Bernie said, "We just grew into it. Being young, we always had ideas about getting more business. We added different products and became a Purina dealer. That added to our volume of business and we just kept growing a little at a time."

But eventually the store needed another full-time employee. So during his senior year at the University of Idaho, Bernie voluntarily ended his college career and returned home to help his parents at the store.

During his time at college in Moscow, Bernie had met his future wife, Helen. When she finished college, her employer transferred her to Boise where, by chance, she attended a dance and ran into Bernie. The two friends became reacquainted, and in 1939, they were married.

In the 1940s, both Bernie and Stanley enlisted in the military. When World War II was over and they returned in 1946, August was ready for them to take over the business completely.

Bernie said, "Our father worried a lot about us boys being in the service. So when we came home, he more or less turned the business over to us. Dad continued to draw a paycheck, but we were all partners and shared in what little revenue there was. There wasn't a lot to go around, but we all managed."

The Company Expands

There were several pivotal events in Zamzows Inc.'s early history. First, the state of Idaho decided to widen Fairview from two lanes to four and make it State Highway 30. That meant Zamzows had to give up the property where the store's gas pumps were. The state didn't want to compensate Zamzows for the loss. After some intense wrangling with the state, Bernie finally secured a substantial payment to make up for the loss of Zamzows' frontage land, as well as the store's gasoline revenue. The state of Idaho's infusion of cash was sorely needed and allowed the company to pay off all of its debts and have some capital for possible expansion.

Zamzows had to decide what to do with the money. They had to decide whether to stay in the feed business or get into the fuel business. At that time, people were starting to convert from coal to oil. Zamzows was dealing coal and had the opportunity to buy an oil distributorship in Boise. They ultimately decided to stay in the feed business and purchased the Meridian Feed Mill in 1953.

But first, Zamzows expanded into the little town of Eagle in 1950. The second Zamzows store was successful, but Eagle's population was only about 300 people. Thus, when the opportunity to buy the Meridian Mill presented itself, Zamzows shut down the Eagle location. The population of Meridian was a little over a thousand when Zamzows bought the mill in 1953. By 1953, the economy was much improved. Bernie sensed it was a good time to expand.

Feed bagger at Zamzows Mill

That expansion proved to be a very smart move.

They changed their milling operations and added a steam roller to the mill. Then they put in a pellet mill and molasses machine to keep up with the times and give the customers, primarily farmers and dairy farmers, the products and services they wanted. As the community grew, Zamzows grew along with it.

The expansion of the Meridian Mill in 1957 was a huge step in Zamzows' growth. Bernie said, "That was our growing pill." But Zamzows was not going into virgin territory. There was plenty of competition in the little town of Meridian.

When the Zamzow family moved to Meridian, there were already eight outlets in town handling feed of some type. They were part of the community and Bernie was told he'd have his hands full trying to compete. But Zamzows did fine because they out-did their competitors, adding new equipment and giving better service. They worked at filling the needs of the community.

The Zamzows purchased another store in 1960: Kuna Mills. Jim and Rick were drafted to help clean up the newly purchased store. "We all went over there and helped clean up that hog house. We cleaned up all the weeds around it and swept the silos. Boy, it was a mess."

Stanley Zamzow was dispatched to run the new Kuna operation, while Bernie oversaw the Meridian Mill and Les Tinkham managed the original store on Fairview.

THAT REMINDS ME OF A STORY

Eventually, Stanley decided to leave the company. Bernie bought out his brother's shares and Stanley invested the proceeds wisely, managing to live well and raise his family without the stresses of owning and managing a retail store.

Carmalita and August at Zamzows mill

In 1978, Bernie sold Zamzows Inc. to his two sons, Jim and Rick. Bernie realized his sons would make changes, but he believed the same philosophy that made him successful at Zamzows would apply to them. "You give the good service the customer wants, you have the character to operate your business honestly, and then you fill the needs of the community and of your customer. With each new generation you bring new ideas and new thoughts into the business. I had different ideas than my parents and my boys have certainly outdone me."

THE HISTORY OF THE FAMILY BUSINESS

Change or Die

Bernie attributed Zamzows Inc.'s success, at least in part, to being able to change with the marketplace. Different eras in history required different strategies.

"Each generation must address the needs of the community they are serving. My dad started out just being a grain grinder and I became more a manufacturer of poultry and livestock feed. And as the lifestyles changed and the territory grew, the farming industry in Ada County disappeared. We either changed or we died. So we got into the garden and pet business and my boys have done very well with that."

Early Meridian Mill before expansion

It takes much more money to operate a business today than it did when Bernie and his parents were running Zamzows. But the basic philosophy is still the same: satisfy the customer, treat them right, and earn their business.

Jim and Rick have followed that philosophy and it's one of the major reasons for their success. Zamzows Inc. has experienced great growth since Jim and Rick took over management of the company in 1978. Bernie pointed out that sales have increased every year since the business began. Bernie said, "I just hope our company is able to continue its growth, support the community, and service them by furnishing their needs."

Original Zamzows store in Kuna

1
Honesty Goes Both Ways

Zamzows Commandment of Good Business #1:

Be honest in all matters. The customer is entitled to full value for his or her dollar.

Hey, Bring My Coal Back!

Zamzows started out in the coal business in 1933. In fact, the first official name of the company was Zamzows Coal and Feed. Getting coal up to the store on Fairview was a problem. It arrived in a coal car at the Hibbards Coal Yard

Zamzows delivery truck

located on 9th Street in the warehouse district of downtown Boise. Zamzows' Fairview store was located in rural Ada County where there were no tracks. That meant someone had to drive a truck to town and hand-shovel the coal from the rail car into the Zamzows coal truck.

In the early days, they used a pitch fork and would be covered with coal dust from head to toe by the time they were done. When Jim and Rick started working at Zamzows in the 1960s, coal was still a major part of the business. It was not unusual for Jim and Rick to each deliver 16 tons of coal a day. Jim said, "You got in a routine and you could shovel two tons of coal into a guy's bin in 15 minutes."

Once a man tried to cheat Jim out of 4,000 pounds of coal. A longtime Zamzows employee at the Fairview store, Ed Havird, had warned Jim to get the money from this man before delivering his coal. Jim went to the man's house, put down his tarp, then went to the door with an invoice and asked the man for payment.

"That's fine, son. You go ahead and start unloading the coal while I make out the check, then I'll bring it out to you."

Jim thought that sounded reasonable, so he started shoveling coal into the man's coal chute. His routine was to shovel two tons of coal, clean his tarp up, and go get paid.

Jim got all the coal shoveled into the man's bin, cleaned everything up, and knocked on the front door. No answer. So Jim went around to the other door and knocked. The man still wouldn't come to the door.

"I knew he was in there, because he hadn't left. There was no way he could have. I was standing there, and he wasn't going to come out and pay me."

Jim knew how to get into any coal bin. He once said he and Rick could have gotten into any house or building in the city through the coal bin. So Jim took his scoop, opened the coal bin, laid out his tarp, and shoveled all the coal back onto the driveway and then into the truck. Then he drove back to the store.

HONESTY GOES BOTH WAYS

The man wasn't happy. By the time Jim got back the man had called and said to Ed, "Hey, bring my coal back! I'll give you the check."

But it was too late. The damage had been done. Jim told Ed, "I will *never* deliver coal to that man. If you want to take coal to that place you're going to have to deliver it yourself, because I'm not taking that SOB one pound of coal."

The man had broken a cardinal rule in dealing with members of the Zamzow family: never take advantage of their honesty. It won't work.

Honesty goes both ways with Zamzows. If Zamzows is ever at fault in any way, they take care of the problem, even when the circumstances may be beyond their control.

When an unscrupulous supplier sold them inferior coal, Zamzows went back to all their customers to voluntarily replace it. There were several different grades of premium coal. The dealer started mixing cheap coal with good coal. Customers were complaining because it wouldn't burn right. When Rick investigated and found out what they were doing, he and Jim spent many weekends shoveling coal out of their customers' bins.

Rick said, "It wasn't our fault, but it wasn't right. We made it right with every single customer."

The bottom line at Zamzows is the customer is entitled to the full value of what they purchased. In the late 1960s and early 1970s when this story took place, this policy was not conveyed with a written guarantee like it is today. But Zamzows stood by their products and their word to their customers. Zamzows is always honest with their customers, and they expect honesty from others in return.

Just Put It on My Tab

Carmalita told the story of an early Fairview customer who used to come in to pick up a bag of Scott's Best Flour. It was old inventory left over from the Snodgrass Mill that Zamzows purchased. The product was kept in the back of the store on a bench near the rear entrance.

Purina feed and checkerboard outside Zamzows store

He would come in and pick up a bag of flour and just walk out the back door with it. August never said anything about it. He knew the man took the flour, so he'd just put it on his bill.

Neither August nor Grandma Z passed any judgment on this man. This was during the height of the Great Depression. Money was tight and people were hurting. As long as they eventually got paid, Zamzows was willing to overlook a customer's peculiar buying habits.

"I thought it was a good way to handle it too," Carmalita said. Confronting the customer would probably have embarrassed him and caused them to lose him for good. Instead, the man and his wife continued to be customers of Zamzows their whole lives. Zamzows likes to give people the opportunity to do the right thing. As long as the customer would eventually pay for what they took, Zamzows was okay with it. Zamzows showed compassion to this man and preserved his dignity by not calling his behavior out, and in doing so, created a loyal customer.

That May Be, But You Still Owe Me $175

"Cool Hand Walt," a longtime Zamzows employee, once collected a bill when even Bernie couldn't. This fellow owed Zamzows $175. Bernie had called the man repeatedly, stopped by his place, and tried almost everything short of a lawsuit. One day, Walt Shepherd, Bernie's right-hand man at the time, said, "Let me give it a try."

According to Jim, Walt and Bernie drove to the man's house and Bernie stayed in the truck while Walt went to the door. As soon as the door opened, the man started yelling, "You low-life, good-for-nothing, cheating, no-account so and so's."

The man railed on for 15 minutes while Walt stood silently and passively. When the man was completely talked out, Walt calmly said, "Well, all of that may be true. But you still owe me $175."

"Yeah . . . I do," said the man. Then he went in and got his checkbook.

Walt Shepherd rarely lost his cool. He understood that patience and respect go a long way. The man wasn't being honest, and Zamzows wasn't going to let him get away with that. Honesty must be upheld on both ends—Zamzows expects to be paid for the good value they provide. But getting others to be honest can be done in a calm and respectful way.

There's Not 100 Pounds in That Sack

One time Bernie Zamzow got in an argument with a customer who said that a 100-pound sack of grain didn't have 100 pounds in it. Zamzows would always put more than 100 pounds in each bag, and Bernie had filled the bag in question himself. But the customer told Bernie, "I'm just paying you for what's in there."

Bernie supervising the installation of the rail spur at the Meridian Mill

At that time, Bernie was a husky young man and handled 100-pound bags routinely. He speculated it might have been because he could pick up that 100-pound sack and set it in the back of his car so easily that the customer somehow thought it was underweight.

When he questioned the weight, Bernie promptly put that bag on the scale and, sure enough, it weighed 103 pounds! But when Bernie held him to his vow to only pay for what's in the sack and told him the price of 103 pounds, he said he was only going to pay for 100. So Bernie opened the bag, removed three pounds, and sewed it back up.

Bernie said, "We always wanted to make sure we gave our customers full value for their dollar." It's a concept that Zamzows has been embracing since 1933 when August and Carmalita started Zamzows during the height of the Great Depression. Grandma Z always insisted that Zamzows would be a business based on honesty.

Counter Check or Sign the Ticket?

In the early days at Zamzows, customers could be trusted to pay. A person's word was their honor. But in the late 1960s things started changing. Boise was growing and some of the people moving into the Treasure Valley had different values than the ones Jim and Rick were raised with. Zamzows soon learned what it was like to be cheated, and had to change their policies accordingly.

Zamzows used to have counter checks for every bank in the area. At the time, nobody carried a checkbook. They'd come in and say, "Give me a First Security check." Then they'd write their name on it and sign it. Or they'd say, "I need 10 sacks of Dairy Feed and I want to sign the ticket." All they had to do was sign the receipt, and it would be placed on a board until they paid.

Cars outside Fairview store in the late 1940s

But around 1965, people quit coming in and paying for the receipts they'd signed. Counter checks began to bounce. Soon Zamzows stopped taking counter checks or allowing people to have credit without a proper application.

But sometimes they still got burned. When Jim and Rick experienced their first big dairy buy-out, they almost went broke. Jim said, "We weren't on top of our accounts receivable and some of our good accounts went south on us." They lost about $30,000 in the 1980s due to bad accounts.

Rick collected nearly $30,000 of almost $60,000 in bad debt that same year by suing one of Zamzows' large customers who refused to pay. Jim Zamzow credits Rick with helping save Zamzows from a potential financial disaster. Rick learned how to do credit and collections early on. "That probably saved our butts," said Jim.

Bernie had told them both, "When you guys open up an account, you have to take the person and explain the terms to them: when it's due and what happens when they don't pay. If they understand that and they sign the application, then you have fewer problems."

Prior to this, a customer could simply ask, "Can I open an account?" Then they'd fill out a form, open an account, and never pay.

Rick said the key is to communicate up front. If you do, you usually end up with a good account. "And that's also true of an employee. If you hire an employee and he or she *knows* where they stand, when the raises will happen, when the review is, and you do what you say you will do, everything works a lot smoother."

The key to a good credit and collection policy and retaining good personnel in any business is *good communication*. Communication helps keep people honest by ensuring that they understand. You can't expect someone to follow rules they don't know exist. Given the opportunity, most people will choose to be honest.

You're About to Meet the Germans

A big city developer from a Greek family with a long, successful history of building shopping centers in many western cities decided to build a new shopping center in Boise. His plan was to hire a local agent to convince the locals to sell their land to him at a low price. The locals could then take their small sums of money and move somewhere else, away from the competition his new shopping center would soon provide. But the local agent soon discovered Rick and Jim Zamzow weren't interested in selling their store.

The agent called on the neighbor who owned the house next to the Zamzows store, which the developer also needed to purchase, telling him he was the only one left who hadn't sold to the developer.

"Even Zamzows?" the neighbor asked.

"Why, yes," said the agent. "The only one who hasn't sold is you."

The neighbor knew Jim and Rick and doubted that story. Telling the agent he'd get back with him, he called Jim Zamzow and confirmed the agent was wrong.

The local agent then called Jim and told him the big city developer had a message for him: "You don't know who you're dealing with. You're about to meet the Greeks."

To that, Jim instructed the local agent to return this message to the developer, "You don't know who *you're* dealing with, because you're about to meet the Germans."

The Zamzow family's German heritage has played an important role in defining who they are. Jim Zamzow described himself like this: "Hard-headed, stubborn, conservative, tremendous work ethic, don't like to be threatened, like to be in control."

Rick Zamzow agreed and said that threatening the Zamzow family is the worst thing you can do. The members of the Zamzow family are stubborn individuals who do not take kindly to having their honesty or their word questioned. One of the surest ways to "meet the Germans" is to be dishonest with a member of the Zamzow family. Honesty is engrained in the very soul of the Zamzow family.

The Greek developer's competing shopping center was built next door, but it hasn't hurt the Zamzows business. In fact, business is booming for Zamzows. The Germans appear to be winning.

Zamzows knows that dishonesty doesn't get you where you want to go. The developer lied in an effort to coerce Zamzows and their neighbor into selling their properties, but in the end, he didn't get either piece of land, and when the new business opened, it wasn't overly successful.

Elvis Was a Narc

In 1970, President Richard M. Nixon made Elvis Presley a Federal Agent-at-Large in the Bureau of Narcotics and Dangerous Drugs. Seven years later, on August 16, 1977, Elvis was found dead in his Graceland Mansion from causes related to the abuse of prescription drugs. Such was the irony of the law enforcement agent who shoplifted from Zamzows.

The man was big and intimidating and worked for a prominent law enforcement agency as the head of their narcotics team. He used his physical size to intimidate people. The man was a regular customer at the Fairview store, shopping primarily for horse items.

Whenever this guy showed up at the Fairview store, merchandise from the horse tack department always went missing. Jim suspected that the man was somehow concealing merchandise and then stealing it, but he didn't know how. So, the next time the guy came into the store, Jim watched him. He saw the man put something from the horse tack department, a silver-inlaid bridle, into his big sheepskin coat and proceed to the checkout counter with another item he intended to buy.

After the man had gone through the register and was walking out the door, Jim asked the cashier, "Did he pay for a horse bridle?"

The cashier said he hadn't, so Jim told the cashier to call the police and then come to the window and watch, because he thought he may need a witness.

When Jim got outside, he stopped the man. "Excuse me sir, but I believe you may have something in your coat that you didn't pay for. Would you mind opening it up so I can take a look?"

HONESTY GOES BOTH WAYS

The man became defensive and refused to open his coat. "Do you know who I am and what I can do to you?" He told Jim he was the head of narcotics enforcement and detailed all the things he could do to him.

But Jim held his ground and told him he still needed to open up his coat because he knew he had something in there from the store and he needed to give it back. When he opened his coat, he showed Jim both sides of it, and it was empty.

Jim was nervous, wondering if he could be wrong. But he knew the man had it in there somewhere, so he held his ground. Jim told him the police were on their way and that they were going to search him and find the item.

The man forced a smile and said, "Okay, here it is. Are you happy now?" He reached into the back of his coat and pulled out a silver horse bridle. It turned out he had a pocket sewn into the back of his coat for the purpose of concealing merchandise.

He handed Jim the bridle saying, "Everything's fine now, right? I can go now?"

Jim said, "No, everything's not fine. You're not going anywhere because the cops are on their way."

By this time, some staff had come out of the store and a few curious customers who witnessed the whole thing. The man knew he was caught. But that didn't stop him from continuing to cause a scene and attempting to use his position of authority along with his physical size to intimidate Jim.

When the police arrived, Jim had the man arrested. Shortly thereafter, the head of the law enforcement agency the man worked for called Jim and asked him what he wanted to do. After all, this was a delicate matter and it would not be good publicity for the agency if the local news were to "go public" with this case. Jim told the shoplifter's boss he wanted the man fired and required to leave the state. The head of the agency agreed, and the man lost his job and left Idaho.

At a Zamzows managers meeting in July of 2003, Jim told that very same story to his eight store managers. He used it to drive home this important point: Zamzows Inc. has as zero-tolerance policy for shoplifters.

THAT REMINDS ME OF A STORY

"Often, the more belligerent a shoplifter is, the guiltier they are. Don't let them intimidate you. They are the guilty ones, not you. They think if they make a big enough scene you'll let them go to avoid the commotion. Don't do it. Have them arrested and prosecute them. This narcotics officer had been stealing from us for quite some time. We'll probably never know how much merchandise this guy stole from us, let alone from other stores in town. If he had a special pocket sewn in his coat to hide things, this was probably not the first time he'd used it. But I made it his last time, at least in this state. And you need to do the same. These people will keep doing this until someone stands up and stops them."

While this story underscores Zamzows' zero-tolerance policy on shoplifting, it more precisely underscores the lesson that honesty goes both ways. Honesty is expected of Zamzows' employees, as well as Zamzows' customers. Telling the story at the managers meeting produced a chilling effect over the managers. They knew Jim was serious about shoplifters, and that dishonesty would not be tolerated at Zamzows.

2

Defend Yourself and What You Love

Zamzows Commandment of Good Business #2:

Be prepared to defend yourself and what you love. You never know what will happen.

Have Gun, Will Travel

As a young man, Jim Zamzow always carried a gun when he traveled—a little .22-caliber automatic pistol—which he kept in his car "just in case." In the mid-1960s, Jim and a college classmate named Cecil went to Tucson, Arizona, for a DECA (Distributive Education Clubs of America, a nonprofit student-run organization) conference and planned on going into Mexico afterward.

Jim was president of the national DECA organization and it wouldn't look too good if his pistol was confiscated by the Mexican authorities when he crossed the border. So, for this trip, he decided not to take it.

They were driving at night to Tucson and scheduled to arrive in Ely, Nevada, by 3 a.m. They reached Bliss, Idaho, around midnight and stopped at the old Y Inn for a cup of coffee and a piece of pie.

When they went to pay, the lady said, "Those two friends of yours who just left paid your tab."

Jim and Cecil didn't know anyone there and were a little astonished. But when they walked out the door two men were waiting for them, one on each side of the door. They both hit Cecil, who fell back and knocked Jim back into the restaurant.

THAT REMINDS ME OF A STORY

Jim and Cecil ran out and got in the car and took off. The two men chased them in their car and tried to run them off the road a number of times between Bliss and Jerome.

Jim Zamzow at age 20

Jim said, "I was just driving for all I had. They'd pull up next to us and swerve to knock us off the road, or they'd pull in front of us and slam on their brakes. Cecil and I were both just praying. We were out in that darn open country and had no way to communicate with anyone. Consequently, I've always felt really vulnerable unless I have a gun with me."

Since that point, Jim has made a point of carrying a gun just in case. He knew this was particularly important when he became the manager of the Fairview store in 1972. He knew a robbery at the store was always a possibility—it's something many businesses have to be prepared for. As a safety precaution, Jim kept a loaded Ruger .44 Magnum single-action revolver in the top right drawer of his desk.

"I wasn't about to give up the money bag without a fight. I realize that attitude is contrary to what you might get from law enforcement nowadays, with the modern mindset being to simply hand over the money so no one gets hurt."

Jim's office sat on the second floor with a one-way glass window looking out over the sales floor. He gave warning to all Fairview store employees, "If I ever kick the glass out of that window, hit the ground! 'Cause I'm fixin' to start shooting."

There was never any question that Jim would defend the property if the need arose. That was why he kept that gun in his desk.

Getting Out of This Office Alive

There are a number of musical unions that represent the writers of song music and lyrics, as well as the publishers of the printed sheet music for guitar and piano. When someone writes a song, they usually license it with one of three organizations, who then collect cash royalties anytime the song is performed. The organization distributes a small portion of these fees back to the writer and publisher after pocketing their portion.

As a result, radio stations pay huge fees for "blanket licenses" each year to all three of these organizations. This covers the fees anytime the radio station plays a song controlled by any of these organizations.

Jim Zamzow thought he was safe playing KYME radio (a local Boise station at the time) in his store in 1974. After all, he advertised on the station. The station had no objection, and, in fact, wrote him a letter giving him permission to play the radio in the store, stating they had already paid the fees to the music union.

THAT REMINDS ME OF A STORY

But soon a local music company that also owned a radio station Jim was *not* advertising on tried to persuade him to pay them a monthly fee to play their music instead of the radio. Jim said no, and they responded by saying that Jim could not play the radio unless he paid the fees they were entitled to.

Whether or not they reported Zamzows to the music union is unknown, but soon Jim began getting letters demanding he either start paying the union or stop playing the radio in the store. The union told him that since Zamzows made money when they were open, playing the radio during business hours qualified as "public performance for profit."

Jim responded with his typical resourcefulness. He simply went out and bought some radios and put price tags on them. After all, Zamzows was a retail store selling a wide variety of products. Why couldn't they sell radios too and have them on to "demonstrate them" to the public? Never mind the fact that they were all tuned to the same station. Plus, if the union representatives came in to the store, they could all be switched off. In fact, for a time there was a sign next to each radio that said, "Not to be played during business hours."

But the union would not give up. Jim felt he was already paying for the radio with their advertising budget, and the station had already paid the fees once. Jim had a letter from Tom Hotchkiss, the KYME manager, saying that he had legitimately paid for his advertising and could play the radio station in the store when the ads were on.

Nonetheless, the music union kept demanding payment. They said, "We sue someone every year, make an example of them, and win every time."

Jim responded, "I just don't think it's right, so I'm going to continue to play the radio in my store."

They continued to send letters, but when that didn't work, they sent a man to Boise who came into Jim's office, sat down in front of him, and started threatening him.

The man began to tell Jim about the kinds of things they would do to him if Zamzows didn't comply. They were more than underhanded threats—they were right out in the open. He said things like, "You'll be lucky if you can get home from the store at night."

So Jim opened his drawer, pulled out his .44 Magnum, and simply laid it on his desk with the barrel pointing right at the man's chest. Then Jim looked him straight in the eye and asked him in a serious tone, "Now let me ask you a question: What makes you think you're going to get out of this office alive?"

The man just turned white. He looked at Jim with astonishment and was probably thinking what a fool this kid was. Jim had not put his hand on the gun or even picked it up, pointed at the man, or threatened him directly with it in any way. He just laid it on the desk with the same kind of veiled threat the union man was giving Jim verbally.

Jim called him on his threats, and the man was absolutely scared to death. He thought Jim was going to kill him. Of course, Jim had no intent to harm him, but his point was apparently well taken: "Don't come in here and try to extort me. The mafia-style tactics might work in New York City, but they won't work here. You guys may kill me, but you aren't going to get what you want because I'm going down with the ship."

Jim Zamzow wasn't about to allow someone to threaten him or his business. He didn't appreciate the dirty tactics, and the gun in the desk came in handy. Sometimes all it takes is the knowledge that you're prepared to defend yourself to make an opponent back down—being prepared pays off.

Not Afraid to Go Hands-On

In the early 1970s, Jim was behind the cash register when a mill worker from Horseshoe Bend walked into the Fairview store and started complaining to Zamzows employee Ed Havird. Jim, who was the newly-appointed store manager, came out and asked, "What's the trouble here?"

"None of your business," was the man's reply.

Jim said, "Hey, what goes on here *is* my business. I'm the manager."

At that, the man took a swing at Jim.

"I pulled my head back and his fist went right past my face. I went around the corner to get him, but my belt loop hooked on a Black & Decker display and threw tools all over the floor!"

Long-term faithful employees Ed Havird (left) and Les Tinkham (right)

Rick walked in holding a clipboard when the punch was thrown, so he dropped the clipboard and took the guy to the ground with a full-nelson wrestling hold and began applying pressure.

The guy's wife was yelling at him and, despite Rick's vice-grip-like hold, the man would not give up.

"If you'll calm down I'll let you up," Rick said. But the man kept fighting and calling Rick and Jim names. So Rick applied even more pressure with the full-nelson until finally the man began whining and eventually started crying. "Quit fighting and I'll let you up." Finally, the man stopped and Rick let him up.

The man almost started another fight, but finally gave up. As to how a younger guy like Rick Zamzow could so successfully take down the logger, Rick explained, "I got him from behind! But it was going to be a mad brawl if somebody didn't stop it."

Jim and Rick have always laughed over that story. The incident has been nicknamed "the customer complaint department."

Jim said, "We've never been afraid to go hands-on if somebody threatens us." You never know what kind of situation you'll find yourself in, especially in a retail store where you see new faces every day. Rick was glad he knew how to defend himself when the man attacked and was able to keep the situation from getting worse.

I Want to Apologize for What I Almost Did

Jim Zamzow started taking karate lessons at age 33. By age 35, he was doing a thousand front kicks a week. He never anticipated he'd have to use these skills. But, when he did, it shook him up.

Jim was at the Fairview store in his office when he heard yelling and obscenities. He got up and walked down to the sales floor where Eric Tabb, a 6-foot-7-inch employee, was having a problem with a "berserk" shoplifter.

This man was yelling obscenities at the top of his lungs to the employees and everyone else in the store. Jim walked up to him and said, "Sir, come back here where I can talk to you."

He said, "I'm not moving," and stood right in front of the glass doors at the front of the store.

Jim told him that if he didn't step away from the doors he was going to have to call the police.

He responded, "You call the police, because I'm not leaving!"

Then Jim made a serious mistake—he turned to walk away and the man attacked him. He hit Jim once right in the back of the head and once on each side of his temple, knocking him down. He was coming at him with a kick when Jim stood up.

THAT REMINDS ME OF A STORY

Jim performing a kata for his wife, Faye

"My people told me what happened next because I went into a certain state where memory ceases and instincts take over. He threw a punch and I blocked it using a technique I'd been studying. Then I hit him with my fist, and my middle knuckle landed right on the bridge of his nose. My knuckle just exploded. I hit him so hard he landed on his shoulders and was blowing blood everywhere when he got up.

"I had already gone into the cat stance. It is a special position you kick from. I had been doing 1,000 front kicks a week and my front kick was very strong. If Kevin Barkell and Bill Precht had not stopped me by pulling me back and grabbing both of my arms, I would have kicked his head right through the glass doors. It was just by grace that they pulled me off."

At this point, Jim called the police. The man went running out of the store, flagged down a police officer on Fairview Avenue, and said he wanted to file assault charges against Jim. But Jim had 10 people who'd witnessed the sequence of events. They found out later that the man was a paranoid schizophrenic who was off his medication.

DEFEND YOURSELF AND WHAT YOU LOVE

There were several interesting twists to this story later that day. Jim had karate training that night so he figured the instructor would want to know all about it. "My adrenalin was still racing when I went to karate class that night and told my instructor about the experience."

Jim said, "Boy, I got into a mess today. Some guy attacked me in the store."

The instructor looked at Jim and said, "Did you win?"

Jim said yes, and the instructor walked away. That was all the attention he gave him over it.

Jim has only used karate defensively and would never dream of hurting anyone with it unless he absolutely had to. The fact that his staff had to pull him off the man scared Jim.

Now keep in mind the man had shoplifted and the police and even his family wanted Jim to press charges for assault and shoplifting. But the reason Jim didn't was that he'd hurt the guy. So, later that night, Jim searched out that man to apologize to him.

Many have asked Jim, "Now why would you do that?"

Jim replies, "It was not because of what he did or even because of what I did. No, I apologized to him for what I *almost* did. Because I almost front-kicked him through that door, which probably would have killed him."

Jim's story shows the importance of showing restraint. Defense is not aggression—in fact, it's meant only to *stop* aggression. Jim took responsibility for his actions, knowing that he'd almost taken it too far. In doing so, he learned the importance of control. While self-defense is important, it should only go as far as it needs to.

Jim said, "I'd like to say what I would do under certain circumstances that haven't happened yet. Boy I think I know. But you don't know how you'll act until you get there."

3

Hard Work, High Standards, No Shortcuts

> Zamzows Commandment of Good Business #3:
>
> Work hard and have quality standards in all you do. Learn from others, but build your own customer base, one customer at a time, whatever way you can.

You Call That Work?

Hard physical labor has been a part of the Zamzow way of life for over 100 years. Jim recalls that even while still in high school, he and Rick did heavy physical labor and thought nothing of it. "We were all strong. We got that way from bucking 100-pound sacks of coal and feed and bales of hay. We'd haul 16 tons of coal a day and have to shovel 10 of that. With 30 pounds on a scoop, it took a while, but we got pretty good at it."

Even so, no matter how hard he and his brother worked, their dad still one-upped them. Jim recalled the time he and Rick stopped at their folks' house after a hard day's work. "Rick and I were black from head to foot. We'd just hauled a record amount of coal and we'd unloaded several railroad cars of slack coal, and when we told Dad about it he said, 'You guys don't work hard. We used to have to unload *lump* coal by throwing it out over the *top* of the railroad car with a pitchfork!'"

Jim and Rick had unloaded the much lighter "slack coal" from the bottom of the railroad car, and not by hand. Jim and Rick augered it off, so all they had to do was shovel it onto the auger. Their dad had them beat on that one.

THAT REMINDS ME OF A STORY

Bernie Zamzow in his garden

A strong German work ethic goes back a long way with the Zamzow family. Some of Grandma Z's earliest memories are helping weed the family garden, where her family got much of their food.

Grandma Z Says . . .

"I grew up weeding onions, and I thought the rows were so long. They wouldn't be long at all, but when you were a kid you'd look down the row and think it was a mile long!"

As the oldest of nine children, Carmalita was expected to help her mother raise her eight brothers and sisters. Carmalita also made most of the family's clothing, from children's underwear to their shirts, pants, and dresses. She became a prolific cook and an expert baker.

HARD WORK, HIGH STANDARDS, NO SHORTCUTS

When she had her own family of five children, she helped milk the cows on the family farm, cook breakfast, and make lunches for everyone in the family. She also worked at Zamzows Coal and Feed during the day, helped do the books in the evening, then stayed up until three or four in the morning baking bread and pies for the next day's lunches.

There's no doubt about it—Carmalita Zamzow set the standard for work in the Zamzow family. And even when she passed away, the headline for the story in *Idaho Statesman* read, "Zamzow Matriarch Epitomized Work Ethic." Truer words were never written.

Carmalita and August Zamzow represented the last generation in America whose goal in life was survival. They got up in the morning and worked so they could eat, clothe themselves, and provide shelter for their family.

Grandma Z used to say, "With a fat hog and if the creek don't rise, we'll make it through the winter."

Grandma Z Says . . .

"My children were lucky to be raised in the period they went through. They learned to work and they learned to do it right. I think that a lot of children today don't have a chance to learn. We still lived the traditional 'old farm' way with everything being done right. And we *insisted* it be done right. And my children, I never did have any problems with them. They knew the work had to be done. They knew we couldn't do it alone, so they knew they had to help. Today's children don't have enough to do, I think. Plus, in the early days, when the children got home from school, we were always home. They'd come running down the road from Cole toward the house yelling, 'Mama, Mama!' They wanted me to know they were home. And it seemed to be very important to them that I was home! I had the same experience with my mother. When I got home from school, she was there. It does make a difference."

No Shortcuts

Jim and Rick Zamzow vividly remember what it was like growing up as Bernie Zamzow's sons. Jim explained, "Pop was strict. He taught us that discipline and hard work were the most important thing. Your job was to get the work done and you could play later. And usually the work never completely got done." Bernie impressed upon his kids that they could always do a better job.

Jim said, "If we cleaned weeds down the fencerow, he didn't come home and say, 'Nice job cleaning the weeds.' He took us out there and showed us what we *didn't* get done. He wanted us to do the job perfectly. He taught us a good work ethic and discipline."

Bernie says he was taught there was only one way to do a job—completely. "Do it the right way and complete it. No shortcuts. If it takes an extra 15 minutes, an extra hour, finish it."

Some of Jim's earliest memories are of work. One of Jim and Rick's first jobs was to push a huge wheelbarrow of manure over a small board that crossed from their yard over to the Fairview store and spread it on the garden.

Jim said, "It took all the strength both of us had just to hold it up, and it still tipped over and manure would go everywhere. That's probably how we learned to haul coal."

Bernie Zamzow was a tough taskmaster and a strict disciplinarian. In fact, Jim chose spending the night in the old Boise City jail over calling his dad.

Rick was a sophomore in high school and was washing the windows at the Meridian store when his dad walked up to him and asked the loaded question, "When did you guys start smoking cigarettes and drinking beer?"

Rick had already noticed that his 18-year-old brother, Jim, had not made it home the previous night, but as Rick put it, "Pop was trying to get me to rat on him, but I couldn't do it. As brothers, Jim and I always stuck up for one another. You have to. It's a sibling thing."

Rick replied to his dad, "Why? What happened?"

Bernie grumbled, "Your brother spent the night in jail. He was arrested for smoking cigarettes and drinking beer."

HARD WORK, HIGH STANDARDS, NO SHORTCUTS

Young Bernie Zamzow

Bernie with Grandma Z

Bernie's garden

Jim was dressed in a suit because he'd been rushing a service club at college. He was drunk, and after a few beers, was feeling sick. He was on Vista at Two Boys In and Out, so he got a cup of coffee, even though he never drank coffee. But he'd heard that coffee would help him to sober up. He was just sitting back at the table when a cop pulled in and arrested him.

The cop took Jim to the police station and said, "You have one phone call. You can call home."

Jim recalls thinking, "No! I'd rather spend the night in jail!"

So he stayed the night in jail. The next morning he went to court. In the courtroom, as he stood in front of the judge, he heard the door open and close behind him, and there was his mother, Helen, coming in.

On the way home, Jim said, "Oh God, Dad's going to kill me."

Helen said, "I'm going to tell you something, but he won't like it very much." She told him a story about Bernie getting drunk his freshman year when he was rushing at the University of Idaho. "A policeman caught him, and he decked the cop."

Bernie denied the part where he "decked" the cop. Either way, it's clear that Bernie's sons knew their dad meant business. While Jim and Rick may not have turned out as strict as Bernie, they certainly inherited his work ethic.

Waste Drives Us Crazy

Jim and Rick Zamzow hate waste. It could be because both their dad and their mom grew up during the Great Depression and passed that mentality on to them. Rick says that his dad used to throw money on the ground and point to it and say, "See that? Well? Aren't you going to pick it up?" When they did he'd grab his money back and tell them, "That's what you're doing when you leave that sack of feed outside where it can get wet and will be ruined. You picked up the dollar bill on the ground a minute ago didn't you? Well, that bag of feed is worth *more* than a dollar and you didn't pick *that* up, did you?"

The message got through loud and clear. Rick and Jim learned never to waste *anything*. Even today, when Jim goes in the company's spacious warehouse, he sees wasteful practices and points them out to the management team. Bernie Zamzow did the same thing. If something was left out or wasted, or a job wasn't done properly, he'd point it out. Jim blames the wasteful practices he sees on the lack of a good work ethic in many of today's youth, and a lack of the type of on-the-job training that both he and Rick experienced.

Waste or not doing a job correctly will never be tolerated at Zamzows. In fact, the Fairview manager joked one day that he didn't need a guard dog to watch the Fairview store. Instead, all he needed was a sign that said, "These premises protected by Bernie Zamzow." There's probably more truth than joke in that statement.

HARD WORK, HIGH STANDARDS, NO SHORTCUTS

Selling Christmas Trees

It was the Christmas of 1972. Jim and Rick had finally convinced their dad to build the new Fairview store. Rick was just married, had quit college, and joined Jim in running the store. They decided to get into the Christmas tree business and had bought a *lot* of fresh Christmas trees. In fact, they had a lot more than they could easily sell.

A man who'd been in the Christmas tree business for years stopped by the store one night and looked the lot over. He came in and said, "Boys, you're in trouble. I've been in this business for a long time and you'll never sell all those trees."

Jim unloading Christmas trees. Each bundle contained four to six trees.

Jim and Rick were scared because they had strict budgets. If they missed one payment, their father was going to shut them down.

1972 was a *very* cold winter. Boise experienced nine days of bone-chilling below-zero temperatures, including a near-record low of 23 degrees below zero. Nevertheless, they stayed out as late as necessary to sell all of the trees.

Jim said, "It got so cold the Christmas trees wouldn't unfold! You know how when they arrive, they come all bundled up? Well, you'd shake them out, and they wouldn't unfold. They were frozen. We had to move them in the store around our displays. We had trees leaning against every display. We'd stay until 10 o'clock at night even if it meant selling just one tree. I accidentally leaned a tree up against the insecticide rack and a bottle of Chlordane got knocked off onto the floor! It was glass so it broke all over the floor. And Chlordane in those days was so powerful it about gassed us out."

Despite the bitter cold weather, the broken bottle of Chlordane, and how scared he and Rick were about not selling all those trees, they did sell most of them and recoup their investment, even though it meant long hours and a lot of extra work.

Zamzows has sold Christmas trees every year since then. However, despite all the planning in the world, every year Zamzows management faces the same challenges Jim and Rick faced in 1972: the weather and tough competitors who are willing to sell their inferior trees for less. The secret then and the secret now is to simply offer better Christmas trees than anyone else and do whatever is necessary to sell every one of them before Christmas.

Getting Customers Any Way You Can

Zamzows has always gone to extraordinary lengths to get customers. Failure wasn't an option. August and Carmalita would sometimes run out of grain and have nothing to sell to local farmers. This frequently happened late in the season, when they didn't have the money to buy large quantities. So they took their little pickup truck and would buy 80 or 100 bags of feed grain from local farmers and resell it.

When Jim and Rick began delivering coal for their dad in the 1960s, they soon learned that their labor was something the customer got for free. The customer paid for the coal—nothing more. If the customer ordered more than their bin would hold, Jim and Rick were taught to take the excess amount off the customer's bill and bring the coal back to the store, even if that meant shoveling the excess coal into the truck to begin with and shoveling it back out when they returned to the store.

"We always took it back, weighed it, and adjusted the bill," Rick said. "You never shorted the customer. It would have been really easy to do but it was never even a consideration."

Jim remembers people coming into the Fairview store in the early 1970s and buying a 15-cent washer for a Hudson Sprayer. "We'd spend a half-hour installing it. We'd literally take their sprayer apart, find the washer that fit, install it, oil it, get it all pumping good, then take them up to the cash register and say, 'That'll be 15 cents,' because that's how much the part was. We never charged to put it on."

Les Tinkham took it one step further by installing axe handles. Someone would buy an axe handle for $1.95, and if he didn't have time to do it at work, he'd take it home at night, put it together, grind it all off, bring it back the next day, and charge them $1.95, which was the price of the handle.

Bernie said, "It's how you got customers." When a customer is treated that well, you have a customer for life. It's part of how Zamzows has been able stay in business and continues to grow even in the age of big box stores. They're willing to do the hard work to earn and keep their customers.

Zamzows derives pleasure from serving others' needs.

4

Going Beyond Expectations

> **Zamzows Commandment of Good Business #4:**
>
> Always do what's best for the customer.
> Go beyond his or her expectations.

The Baker's Dozen Concept

Jim Zamzow believes customer service is in the blood of the Zamzow family. As part of his strict German upbringing, Jim was taught to be a servant, to work beyond what he was paid to do and expect no extra compensation. This strong German work ethic was part of the Zamzows policy to always provide the customer with extra value—the concept of the baker's dozen. It applies to all things in life.

"My dad always told me to do more and give more than what you are paid for. If you are hired for five dollars an hour to do an hour's worth of work, give your boss an hour and 15 minutes for those five dollars. If you are paid from 8:00 to 5:00, be at work by 7:30, work until 5:30, and get paid from 8:00 to 5:00. Always do extra. And if you ever want to go get a job someplace and it's difficult to get that job, tell the boss that you are willing to work for free to prove your worth. Guarantee you are going to be worth his money."

Zamzows applies this lesson to its products. They guarantee their products are going to work. Jim says, "If they don't work, then we are selling the wrong product and we don't want to sell it. Always give a little bit more than what you're being paid for. That's the baker's dozen concept. That's the way our business was developed."

Zamzows has always gone out of their way to ensure the customer gets full value, plus some. Even when things were hard, Zamzows has always given their best service to their customers.

Portable feed mill at Meridian Mill

The winter of 1972-1973 was a cold one in Boise. Temperatures were well below zero for a number of days in a row. It was mid-December and Rick Zamzow had just gotten out of college and married his high school sweetheart, Roxanne Reed, in November. The couple lived in a small house by the Union Pacific Railroad Depot. It had been a tough year. The nation and the Boise area were both in an economic recession. Money was tight and Zamzows had just built their new Fairview store.

The company had bought an oil truck, used to deliver fuel to local homes and businesses. Many homes in Boise that originally heated with coal had converted to oil. It was the day before Christmas, and Rick had been out in the oil truck from about 6 a.m. until 8 p.m.

It was so cold that everyone was running out of oil. The oil wouldn't pump very well either. It was like molasses. They'd have to mix in stove oil, which was the next grade up from standard heating oil. Rick was completely exhausted and hadn't had a day off for about two weeks.

It was Christmas morning and he received a call from a man who was out of oil. Rick went to his parents' house and said, "I've got a customer that's out of oil. But I don't know what to do about it." It was Christmas, and he was sick of pumping oil.

But Bernie said, "Get that thing fired up and we'll all go do that before we open presents!" So Rick, Jim, and Bernie all jumped in the oil truck. The elderly man to whom they delivered the oil was in tears. There were the Zamzows postponing their Christmas to deliver oil so a family could stay warm.

Rick said, "That's just how we were raised. You took care of your customer."

The Zamzows felt they were lucky to have *any* customer. Jim said, "Even if we were closed and putting things away and somebody would pull up to see if we were still open, we'd run out and wave at them and say, 'Come on in.' They'd pull over say, 'But you're closed.' And we'd say, 'No. Come on in. What do you need?'"

There would often be a livestock sale at one of several nearby stockyards that ended at 5 p.m. on Saturdays. At that time, the Zamzows stores closed at 5 p.m., as did most businesses in the Treasure Valley. Even though they were supposed to be closed, Zamzows always stayed around for an extra hour to take care of anyone who had purchased a young calf, lamb, or other animal that needed milk substitute.

As times changed in Boise, Zamzows changed as well. With changing work schedules and different lifestyles, Zamzows must base their schedule on the needs of the customer. They're willing to put their own interests aside to help people when they need it.

Don't Put Sheeze on It Unless They Ask

There was an old German professor at the University of Idaho who had a standard order at the student union restaurant. Bernie was working his way through college at the restaurant, known as the old Blue Bucket.

The professor always came in a few minutes early because he wanted to avoid the rush, and he always sat in the same place.

When someone took his order he would say, "Bring me a slice of apple pie with a piece of sheeze on it, and a cup of coffee!"

On a particularly busy day, the professor came in, and Bernie thought they were about to be hit with a rush. So he grabbed a cup of coffee and got him a slice of apple pie, put the cheese on it, and took it to him. After all, that was what he always ordered.

But when he set it down on the table in front of him, the professor said, "What's this?"

Bernie replied, "This is what you always get."

The professor said, "Bring me a menu!"

Bernie had to take the pie and coffee back. That incident taught Bernie not to take your customers for granted. It's best to let them tell you what they want rather than assuming you know.

Load This Feed or Shove It

When Jim and Rick took over Zamzows in 1970, there was a lot to learn. The company was in the process of building a new store on Fairview Avenue. For a time, the old store building remained standing in front, while the first new structure to be occupied was the just-completed warehouse out back. Jim and Rick were working out of the new warehouse when they got into a struggle with feed customers who still wanted to go to the old store.

Jim said, "I thought I could train people by encouraging them to go to the big warehouse door instead of blocking the two walk-in doors of the old building."

One fellow pulled up and parked in front of the walk-in doors. Jim said, "If you'll just pull over to that big door."

The man replied, "I'm parked right there in front of those two walk-in doors. Just throw it in my truck right there."

Jim insisted, "If you'll just pull right over here, I'll load it up for you."

"I'm not going to do it."

"Well, that's where we load our feed," Jim told him.

"If you won't take my feed and throw it into my truck where it is right now, you can shove it!" said the man.

Jim replied, "Yes, sir."

Jim learned a lesson in that moment: you make shopping convenient for the customer, not yourself.

A few years later, when the new front portion of the Fairview store had opened, Jim was still trying to train the customer. Again, it didn't work. He wanted to have customers park in front of the store and not walk through the warehouse.

Rick said, "We didn't want people coming in the back way because Les Tinkham would load their feed without a receipt and then they'd drive off. Les insisted that he load the feed when he was out there. So, we tried to force the customer to not park in the back and walk through the warehouse."

After about the fifth customer got mad at Rick, he went to Jim and said, "We can't keep customers from walking through this warehouse. They are going to park here and walk through."

Jim said, "No, we have got to do it like that."

It took them a while to figure out that they needed to do what the customer wanted. When they did, they completely changed their philosophy. Then they would ask the customer, "Would you like that brought out front or would you like to pull around back?"

When Jim and Rick started doing it the customer's way, everything went smoothly.

Earning Your Own Customers

Both Jim and Rick Zamzow had tremendous admiration for Union Farm and Garden on Orchard Street. In the late 1960s and early 1970s, Union Farm and Garden was the largest and most successful garden store in the state of Idaho. So Jim and Rick convinced their dad to borrow the money and build a brand-new Fairview store. They reasoned, "If we build it, the customers will come." Unfortunately, the brothers soon found out it wasn't that easy.

Jim and Rick would sit at the store, ready for a busy Saturday, but they had no customers. So Jim would say, "Let's go over and see how many customers are at Union Farm and Garden." They'd then drive over to Union Farm and Garden, but were scared to go in because they were spying.

They'd sit and watch from the parking lot of the little strip mall across the street. One Saturday, Rick sent Jim over to see what was going on. There wasn't a single open parking spot in their lot.

Zamzows Fairview storefront in the early 70s

Rick asked, "Were they busy?"

Jim had to tell him, "You couldn't even get in their parking lot."

They learned the basis of success from Union Farm and Garden. Jim said, "What we learned was we couldn't get their customer. Once a business is established and they're taking good care of them, the customers don't want to shop anywhere else. So we weren't going after their customers. We thought we were, but in reality, we had to build a whole new customer base."

There was a good reason behind Lester McCraken and Union Farm and Garden's success. They knew the lawn and garden business. Rick said, "The reason they were shopping at Lester McCraken's was because he knew the answers. He was a problem-solver. We could solve your horse problems, rabbit problems, 'most any animal problem, but we didn't know the lawn and garden business. Of course we knew how to plant a garden. We knew we had to fertilize with natural manure before we planted every spring. What we didn't know was the business side of lawn and garden. So Jim and I realized we had to learn the lawn and garden business."

So they learned it, sometimes by accident, and sometimes in the course of doing something Zamzows had been doing for years. One of the things that Zamzows had done almost from the beginning was deliver coal. That gave Jim and Rick the idea of using their coal trucks to deliver Soil-Aid mulch in the spring and summer. But how do you get customers to try a new product they'd never even heard of?

Both Jim and Rick Zamzow remember that one of the best ways they first got Soil-Aid customers and lawn and garden customers in general was the "feed tag trick."

It was the first ad they ever ran. They took old feed cards and had a printing company put a big red question mark on them along with the words "Planting a new lawn? See us for all you need. Zamzows 6313 Fairview Ave. Phone 375-4231."

Then they stapled a little plastic bag of Soil-Aid to the cards and left one at every door. Newly constructed homes were a prime target. They'd pass out the tags in neighborhoods, or they'd see a bad lawn and knock on the door. "Pardon me sir, we're sorry to bother you, but do you realize your lawn has some billbug damage? This is what you need to do. Zamzows is here to serve you."

It worked fantastically. Jim said, "Whenever Rick or I would go out to deliver Soil-Aid into one of these new subdivisions in the early 1970s, there would be 20 or 30 houses where a lawn hadn't been planted yet. We'd just stop at every house and leave one of those flyers with the little bag of Soil-Aid. We got a tremendous response! People called and said, 'Hey, we need help planting our lawn! We don't know how to do it. What do we do?'"

Jim and Rick learned that the best way to find customers was to earn them. Union Farm and Garden earned their customers through their knowledge of the garden business. Zamzows would have to simply work hard at developing their own customer base. So Jim and Rick went to work and began to earn their own customers through the merit of their good service and quality products.

99-Cent Steer Manure

In the early 1970s, national and regional stores like K-Mart and Sears began to carry lawn and garden products. K-Mart offered cheap products like 77-cent garden hoses and rakes. Both stores began to compete fiercely with Zamzows on bagged steer manure, something Zamzows sold in large quantities but at modest profit margins.

When K-Mart's and Sears' lower price on bagged steer manure began to hurt their sales, Zamzows decided to take them head-on and bring in a truckload of the stuff. Handling steer manure, even small amounts, is hard and unpleasant work. In those days, bagged steer manure stunk terribly and was not good compost. Processing manure to be odor-free wasn't widely done at the time.

In the early 1970s, Zamzows was still trying to figure out who they were and what kind of store they wanted to be. Zamzows liked selling high quality goods. The strategy in bringing in a truckload of steer manure was not just to compete with Sears and K-Mart, but to bring traffic into the store. After all, Jim reasoned, when the K-Mart customer showed up for their bag of 99-cent steer manure, they'd see Zamzows' high quality goods and gladly pay a few dollars more to get a better quality rake as well, right? Wrong.

Jim recalled, "We were trying to get the K-Mart customer to quit K-Mart and come to Zamzows. We had dropped our image way down and we got that level of customer, but they're a different breed of cat. They'll drive over a rake with their car and expect you to replace it. They'll break the cheap hose and want it replaced. And while they were at the store, their kids would knock stuff off the shelves, their dog would pee on the wall, and the parents would probably steal something! I'm being a bit facetious of course, but that's the customer we'd attracted. We realized we were attracting a clientele we didn't want! We wanted customers who appreciated good service and high quality, not just cheap."

When Jim brought in an entire truckload of bagged steer manure and sold it for 99 cents a bag, it went well. Perhaps *too well*. Zamzows sold tons and tons of it. People would back up and fill up their cars with it. But it was a loss/leader item and it took all of the employees' time just to load it, while customers in the store needing service had to wait.

To make matters worse, Jim was in his office and Rick got stuck loading bags of steer manure all day long. And the next time he saw Jim, words were exchanged.

He came to Jim and said, "I've loaded my last sack of 99-cent manure. I'm not going to waste my time loading manure when people need my help inside, but I can't help them because you've got me out there loading steer manure, which we don't make any money on anyway!"

Jim and Rick have taken this lesson to heart and have focused on developing products which successfully address their quest for quality. Price has not proven to be a stumbling block for any of Zamzows' proprietary products.

5

Finding New Products and Ideas

Zamzows Commandment of Good Business #5:

Be innovative. Search out and develop new ideas and products, and then have the courage to stick with them.

Empty Coal Trucks and Soil-Aid

In the 1960s, The Boise Cascade Saw Mill in Emmett had a lot of surplus tree bark. They'd strip the bark off the logs they cut into lumber and grind it up. They'd add nitrogen to the bark to make it decompose quicker because all they really wanted to do was dispose of it.

Zamzows was starting to sell a lot of lawn seed during Boise's housing boom of the late 1960s and early 1970s and Jim and Rick figured out that decomposing bark made great mulch to cover newly-planted lawns. They used the bark from the saw mill and called the new product Soil-Aid.

They didn't invent Soil-Aid, but Zamzows was one of the first to sell it in Boise. Zamzows trucks would deliver coal from October until April, but they weren't used during the rest of the year. So Zamzows started using the coal trucks to haul this new product. They'd send the trucks to Emmett, pay Boise Cascade Saw Mill a small fee to do the loading, and sell the Soil-Aid in Boise and Meridian.

Zamzows had always sold peat moss, but this composted bark was perfect to cover grass and use in flower beds. It was a genuine *soil-aid*. It actually improved the soil. Later, Boise Cascade named it Soil-Aid and eventually started selling ground bark. They continued to call it Soil-Aid, even though it was fresh, raw ground bark and still had some wood in it. There was a big difference between that and the product Zamzows sold. But the mill's line of Soil-Aid was discontinued when they shut down their Emmett mill, while Zamzows continued to sell their high-quality product.

The sawmill in Emmett, Idaho (Courtesy Idaho State Archives)

The boys found a way to take advantage of resources that weren't being used to their full potential and offer a new, quality product. Zamzows is always on the lookout for new products, and if they can reduce waste and enrich the earth while they're at it, that's all the better.

False Chinch Bug and His Cousin Bill

The bluegrass billbug was not all that common in the Boise area. Zamzows had rarely heard of them when billbugs first began to hit Ontario, Oregon, in the 70s, gradually eating their way to Boise.

The adult billbug was small and didn't cause a real problem. But by the time you could see the adults, the larvae they had evolved from had already chewed all the roots off your lawn, leaving behind brown grass so dead it would simply pull out easily. At first, folks thought their lawns weren't getting enough water. Soon, however, the brown spots wouldn't go away no matter how much they were watered.

Zamzows was the first to identify billbugs in the Treasure Valley and discovered that the powerful chemical, Chlordane, would kill them. When the bluegrass billbug seemed to become resistant to Chlordane, Zamzows pioneered other chemical and organic ways to kill them, including the use of beneficial nematodes. In fact, Zamzows became innovators, not only in finding the cure, but in identifying yard-related problems in the first place. For example, Rick noticed some small bugs in his yard and thought he had billbugs, so he gave the lawn a heavy spray of Chlordane. A bunch of tiny bugs came running out of his lawn and onto the sidewalk.

Neither Jim nor Rick knew what they were, but photos in a reference book made them think they were dealing with some type of chinch bug. So they called Dorn Peterson, the County Agent at the time, but he said, "No, we don't have chinch bugs here."

They ended up sending some of the "mystery pests" to an entomology lab at Penn State University. The response said, "You have what is known as a *false* chinch bug."

"What is the difference?" asked Jim and Rick.

Penn State replied, "They do exactly the same thing as a true chinch bug. Both suck the plant, poison it, and the leaf dies."

"So we became innovators instead of just me-toos," Jim said. These important discoveries point to why Zamzows has become Treasure Valley's lawn and garden leader, replacing Union Farm and Garden as the state's largest independent store of its type. Zamzows is willing to do the research to identify problems and innovate solutions.

Time for a New Weed Eater

In the late 1970s, Jim Zamzow took his family to the Oregon coast on vacation. Driving back, they stopped near Bend at a resort called Sun River. The kids were small at the time and Jim's wife, Faye, had made some tuna sandwiches for the trip. They stopped at a park to eat and let the kids play.

There, Jim noticed a park maintenance guy trimming around some lava rocks. He appeared to be using a long-handled trimmer with a big blade on the end of it, like the ones Zamzows sold. Jim watched him trim and told Faye, "You know, that guy is the best with that tool that I have ever seen. He is getting close enough to those weeds to trim them yet he's never hit the rock once!"

Jim couldn't believe it. He sat there and ate his sandwich until the gardener stopped for lunch and leaned his machine up against a rock. Jim went over to look at his tool to check his blade and see how badly it was worn and was surprised to find fishing line where the blade should have been!

"No wonder he's not getting any sparks," said Jim. "What a great idea." He wrote down the name of the tool. Until then, the stores had been selling battery-operated hand trimmers which used a back-and-forth motion. Those were an improvement over the old scissors-style hand trimmers, but this was something completely different.

The trimmer Jim had seen in Sun River was marketed only to professional users like parks departments. Six months later, while in Hawaii on vacation, he saw an ad for a Weed Eater-brand trimmer that had just been introduced for sale to the general public. There was only one model at that time. It was big, green, and had a three-quarter horsepower motor.

How do you market a brand new product that no one has ever seen? Jim's plan was to introduce it to folks the same way he'd first seen it, in action. Better yet, he let people experience it for themselves.

They set one of the line trimmers up and took customers next door to the old motel and let them trim weeds around the trees. They sold one to almost every person who tried it.

Zamzows is always looking for the next "Weed Eater"—a product that will revolutionize the way something is done. The key is to be early in the market to sell the new product. Like the Weed Eater, it's taken some national stores more time to figure out what Zamzows already knows. One local store seems to watch what Zamzows buys, then simply brings in the same items and sells them for a little less. The big box stores are often able to sell the product for less

FINDING NEW PRODUCTS AND IDEAS

than Zamzows pays to buy it. When that happens, Zamzows stops selling the product and starts looking for another "Weed Eater."

The Solution to the Farming Problem

Jim Zamzow wanted to develop a line of environmentally-sound products that would be competitive with chemical fertilizers. Jim knew that composted manure would be a big improvement over chemical fertilizers. What he didn't realize was how much it would cost.

Jim invested in his research

Duane Yamamoto, the former Mayor of Kuna, intended to plant 640 acres of sugar beets south of Kuna. Jim wanted to suggest he put down some composted manure in lieu of chemical fertilizer.

"Duane, what you ought to do is put 20 tons of good compost per acre on that alkali ground and till it in."

"Really?" said the mayor. He knew it would be too expensive but acted interested. "Do me this favor and I'll go along with you. Find me enough compost to put on 20 tons per acre, show me the economics of getting it delivered, applied, and worked into the soil, and if I can do it for anywhere close to what I'm spending on chemical fertilizer, I'll go for it."

It was no easy task. No one even composted manure in those days. There was only raw manure available. And when Jim started calling around to dairy farms and other potential sources, he discovered there wasn't enough manure in all of Ada County to do what he wanted. On top of that, there was the matter of having it delivered 10 miles south of Kuna and spreading it on the ground.

When Jim told Duane the bad news, Duane said, "I already knew that, but I didn't think you did. So, by giving you that homework assignment, I knew you'd learn that too."

Then Duane Yamamoto said something to Jim that would send him on a 20-year search for the perfect fertilizer. "Let me tell you something, young man. If you could ever come up with something that did for the soil what that 20 tons of composted manure would do, but you could make it economical enough for us to buy it and easy enough to apply, you'd have the solution to the farming problem."

That challenge planted the seed in Jim's mind that he worked on for about 20 years. It was ultimately how he came up with the product Zamzows called Save-a-Tree, or Thrive.

Zamzows knows the value of finding and creating new products, and they're always looking for better and more effective ways to do things.

It's Dynamite!

Bernie worked with a man who formulated a product to supplement racehorses. One day, Jim asked him, "Dad, I remember you used to make a racehorse supplement. Whatever happened to that?"

He said, "Oh, that was old Cliff Hensley." Hensley was a pharmacist. "We formulated that, and he did really well with it, and then Cliff had a stroke. That was pretty much the end of it."

Jim asked, "Do you still have the formula?"

"I've got it somewhere."

"Would it be okay if we used it?"

He said, "Oh yeah. It wasn't trademarked or anything. Cliff and I just put it together and it worked really well. In fact, a lot of Kentucky Derby winners were fed that product."

So Jim got the formula and looked it over. He said, "I might as well have been reading Russian because I didn't understand any of it." He figured the only way he would learn to understand it was if he started with the first ingredient: vitamin A. So he learned everything he could learn about vitamin A. Then he moved on to vitamin D, then E. He learned all about the fat-soluble vitamins and then all the water-soluble vitamins. Then he tackled the minerals.

Jim created a formula that he called Formula 8-12, made for racehorses, as well as Formula 8-15. Both were named for the dates they were finished, a choice Jim made so he could go back through his records in case he needed to cross-reference the formulas.

Jockeys Gary and Scott Stevens carried the products to Louisiana Downs and San Anita and other big races. But soon Bernie's formulator didn't want to make the products anymore because Jim could only sell 200 pounds of the product a year. He said, "I'm not going to make that 8-15 for you anymore. I can't clean all the equipment out just to make 200 pounds in a two-ton mixer. If you can't take two tons, then I'm not going to make it for you anymore."

Jim wondered how he could bring sales up enough to get the formulator to continue producing the product. So he started a multi-level marketing company to sell the supplement.

Jim was contacted by a woman who introduced him to Kirby Buchanan, actor and racehorse enthusiast, over the phone. Then Jim flew down to L.A., where he toured racetracks with Kirby and the two of them became great friends. Kirby became a representative for the product line. That was how Jim got into the racehorse business.

Eventually the supplement morphed into the product called Dynamite. The name came about through a fellow by the name of Orville Horst. Jim would create a formula and would hand blend it and then give it to several guys with racehorses, including Orville. They'd try it on their horses and tell him what the products did, whether they made the horse too hot or too sleepy or something else. Jim knew what he'd done to the products, so he knew how to tweak them.

Finally Orville came in one day and said, "Jim, that last formula, it's dynamite!"

Jim immediately filed for that name and changed it from Formula 8-15 to Dynamite Performance. The product line has since expanded with the help of the multi-level marketing company and now feeds hundreds of thousands of horses.

Horses fed Dynamite have won just about every major horse athletic event in the world. Jim founded his multi-level marketing company for horse supplements in 1982. They call Dynamite the horse industry's best-kept secret because most of the big horse-nutrient products sell through stores, but Jim's products don't. They sell directly through horsemen, and as a result they're able to penetrate the market in a way that other products can't.

Swift and Sweet

A fellow by the name of Sonny Olson, who was a greyhound breeder in Kansas, called Jim one day and said, "You know, I really like your product Dynamite. But I don't know how much to feed my dogs."

Jim was confused. He didn't have a dog product. He asked, "What are you talking about?"

Sonny said, "Your horse supplement. I'm just kind of guessing. How much should I feed my dogs?"

Jim replied, "That's not formulated for dogs."

"Well it works pretty well with them, but what do you think I oughta feed them?"

Jim thought about it and said, "Sonny, let me study greyhound blood types." Greyhounds are different than other dogs, and Jim wanted to make sure he was doing the right thing for the dogs. So he went through the same process he had with the Dynamite formula, giving Sonny the formula and getting feedback on what it did to his dogs.

FINDING NEW PRODUCTS AND IDEAS

Finally, when Jim hit on the right ingredients, Sonny said, "All these other guys selling greyhound supplements, we ought to call them and tell them we want a showdown."

Jim said, "Sonny, can I have that name?"

"Sure."

So Jim trademarked Showdown. After Sonny had been feeding the product to his dogs for almost two years, he called Jim. "Jim, this stuff is just incredible. I have a bitch that had five puppies and they're all stakes dogs."

"Nice," said Jim. "That sounds pretty good."

He said, "Wait a minute, that sounds *pretty good*? Do you know what I just said?"

"Yeah, they're all good dogs."

"No, you're a horse guy. Let's just say you have a mare and a stallion and you get five foals and they all run in Kentucky Derby. These are all stakes dogs, all champions, all five of them! I've got the mama and I've bred her back to one of our stud dogs. And I'll tell you something about your product—your product doesn't even completely genetically come to fulfillment until the third generation of both the stud and the bitch. They just keep getting better and better and better. I've got the puppy that is the pick of the litter and we've named her Swift and Sweet. Do you want her?"

Jim said, "I don't even know what I would do with her. We don't race greyhounds."

He said, "No, no, no. I'd keep her. I'd train her. I'd race her. You finance her."

"Thanks, but no."

Swift and Sweet went on to set records in all of the tracks that she raced in. Sonny later asked Jim what he thought about Swift and Sweet, and Jim said, "You know, I've made a lot of mistakes, and that's just one of them."

The story of Showdown, like the story of Dynamite, shows why it's worthwhile to put in the work and research to develop your own brands and pioneer new products and find unique ways to sell them. Jim paid attention to the market and formulated his products based on the customers' specific needs, and Showdown and Dynamite have both been great successes.

THAT REMINDS ME OF A STORY

Pioneering Premium Pet Food: The Iams Story

Since the company began in 1933, Zamzows has pioneered a lot of dog and cat foods. Grocery store dog and cat foods were not common in the 1930s and 1940s. Zamzows brought in Purina Dog Chow, Wayne Dog Food, and a few others. But the most significant product category Zamzows pioneered was premium pet foods.

Using the latest scientific formulas, Zamzows had been making their own animal feeds since 1933. However, the mill in Meridian didn't have the sophisticated equipment required to produce commercial pet food. Making dog and cat food required a multimillion-dollar plant with an extruder to create pressure-cooked pet food in small nuggets. Purina started the trend in 1950 when they introduced the first pressure-processed dog food. Other companies quickly followed. Zamzows did make a pelleted dog food in 1974 for farm dogs, which sold quite well. But Jim and Rick were looking for something better.

Iams feed dumped outside delivery door

FINDING NEW PRODUCTS AND IDEAS

In the early 1970s, Hill's Science Diet was selling scientifically formulated dog foods exclusively through veterinarians. The Hill's Pet Nutrition Company goes back to 1943 when Dr. Mark L. Morris, Sr. believed certain diseases in pets could be managed through carefully formulated nutrition. When a blind man named Morris Frank asked Dr. Morris if anything could be done to save his guide dog who was suffering from kidney failure, the result was a pet food for dogs with kidney disease that was available by prescription only. Jim and Rick Zamzow took note and when Hill's developed a nonprescription formula, they asked Hill's for permission to become the first non-veterinarian retailers in United States to sell it.

They finally talked them into it but, six months later, Garden Center West was also stocking it. Zamzows had been buying Science Diet through a distributor in Montana who told them, "If you want a premium dog food, you don't want Science Diet. You want Iams."

Animal nutritionist Paul Iams founded the Iams Company in 1946 in a small feed mill near Dayton, Ohio. The story goes that Iams visited a mink ranch and saw a very old dog with an incredibly shiny coat running around like a puppy. He asked what the dog was eating and found out it was the same thing they were feeding the mink. From that formula, he developed what was at that time the world's best pet food. Jim and Rick wanted to try it, so they had the distributor in Montana send them some.

They bought five tons that first year but only sold one ton. The other four tons got wormy and were ground up into hog food. Compared to what Zamzows was carrying, Iams Dog Food was just too expensive. Jim said, "Iams was $7.95 for 20 pounds and we were selling 50 pounds of Purina Dog Chow for $3.95!" Jim called a meeting of the Zamzows board of directors to plead his case for keeping the line.

Jim was fighting with the board because the customers who were feeding their dogs Iams kept saying, "Don't quit it." The board agreed reluctantly and Jim brought in another five tons. The distributor sent it via an independent trucker who arrived on Sunday morning while Rick was having coffee with his parents. The trucker backed the truck up, opened the door, and dumped five tons of premium dog food in the parking lot.

When Rick went over to the store and found bags of dog food in the parking lot, he was mad. Jim said, "I don't know if he thought I did it or was just unhappy that it had showed up in the first place, but when I got there he chased me around the parking lot with a feed cart!"

After that, Jim and Rick came to an understanding. They would communicate with one another before they got angry and there would be no more chasing one another around the parking lot. Rick later said, "It's a good thing he could outrun me. Ultimately, Iams became a huge seller for Zamzows."

Jim's vision was profitable and was the basis for many premium formulations to come. The Iams story shows the importance of selling quality products even when it's not easy. It may take a lot of work initially, but it pays off in the end.

6

If You Want to Do It Right, Make It Yourself

> **Zamzows Commandment of Good Business #6:**
>
> Develop your own superior brands so you can control the quality and protect your market.

Zamzows' Product Development for Others

Despite what Jim and Rick learned from their mentors, they also found out that depending on other people's products for Zamzows' success has its pitfalls. Zamzows has often been the first local retailer to take on a new product. Many times they were promised exclusive rights to a product in the Boise area. Then, for a variety of reasons, the product ended up at Zamzows' competitors.

Zamzows would identify the need for a new product or discover a product they think would be beneficial to their customers. Then they bring in that new product, learn how it works, train their staff on how to use it, and advertise it. The manufacturer, seeing how well the product is doing for Zamzows, would break their word and take it to Zamzows' competitors, who could sell it for less since Zamzows already did the groundwork. The manufacturer, now tasting some degree of success, would abuse their position of trust with the customer and cheapen the quality of their product.

This scenario has happened time and time again at Zamzows. Bernie Zamzow said, "The reason we got away from Purina and went back to Zamzows feeds was because Purina was shortcutting us. But at the time, we didn't learn. We developed Wayne Dog Food for Allied Mills, then they backtracked on what they'd promised us. The pattern repeated itself with Iams and others. Finally, we learned the lesson: there's only one way. You *must* develop your own products so no one can take them away from you or erode the market."

The Purina Story

One of the biggest advancements made by the Fairview store was when they took on the Purina line and became a Check-R-Mix dealer. The Purina Company started making animal feed pressed into small cubes, known as pellets, in 1921. Purina founder, William Danforth, replaced the word "feed" with "chow." Danforth had noticed how soldiers in World War I responded to the word chow while he served as YMCA secretary for the troops of the Third Army Division in France. Purina Chows were sold at Zamzows as early as 1944 with the installation of a new mixing machine at the Fairview store.

Purina checkerboard on early Zamzows Fairview storefront after expansion of Fairview Avenue

IF YOU WANT TO DO IT RIGHT, MAKE IT YOURSELF

In the early days, Purina was a highly respected company. They did it right. They taught all their dealers how to sell Purina products through slide shows. Jim recalls that there would be a scratchy old record playing a voice track with slides up on the screen. A bell would ring to tell the projector operator when to change the slide.

Along with education of their dealers' employees, Purina did a lot of other innovative things that Zamzows would later emulate. In 1926, Purina Founder William Danforth's son opened the Purina Pet Care Center for the purpose of research and testing new and existing Purina products. This helped lead to the development of Purina Dog Chow, which was instrumental in Purina's success. But Purina's success with Zamzows would not last.

Zamzows was a successful Purina dealer—perhaps too successful. In the 1940s, being a franchised dealer of Purina Check-R-Mix feeds meant your entire identity became Purina. Zamzows was no exception and the Fairview store, and soon the new Meridian Mill, were both painted with the familiar red and white checkerboard design of Purina. Zamzows store calendars proudly touted the Purina logo. Even in their early phone book ads in Boise and Meridian, Zamzows *was* Purina.

Purina had been selling dog food for farm animals through rural feed stores like Zamzows since 1926. So, when Purina Dog Chow was introduced in the early 1950s, Zamzows was one of the first stores to get on board. Both Bernie and Stanley Zamzow recommended the food to their customers and did large displays in both stores to promote sales of the new product. It worked, and soon Zamzows was doing a brisk business in Purina Dog Chow.

But in 1957, Purina took the popular dog food into the grocery store, and Purina was soon selling dog food in Albertsons and Safeway stores throughout the Boise Valley. Zamzows had just lost the market they helped develop. And Purina was also taking their feed customers.

But once Bernie had established a market for Purina's products, Purina felt that market belonged to them, not Zamzows. And when they were ready, Purina simply took it away. Zamzows would develop customers. They'd sell entire railroad-cars of cattle feed pellets to the feed lots. Then Purina started taking them away by selling direct.

In the 1960s, Purina began to lower the quality of their feeds through lowest-cost formulation. Purina's priorities had changed from that of serving their customers to serving their shareholders. In 1963, Ralston Purina Company acquired Van Camp Sea Food Company. In 1968, they bought Foodmaker and Jack in the Box restaurants and, a year later, Keystone Resorts. These acquisitions cost Purina a lot of money, so they were in no mood to let anyone keep more of their profits than necessary, even a little dealer like Zamzows.

Rick said, "It was the same old problem. We'd develop their product only to have them take it away from us."

Jim pointed out that Purina would not let Zamzows carry any product that competed with a Purina product, even if it was superior. "We brought in Blue Mountain Super Meat, which was a very good dog food. They said we couldn't do that. We tried making our own horse feed and they said we couldn't do that either."

It finally came to a head when Purina presented Bernie with this ultimatum: sell the entire line of Purina products, or sell none at all. Bernie simply said, "To hell with you."

This story made quite an impression on Rick, who was still in school at the time. "That took some real courage," he said. "Purina was a large part of our business." Zamzows had all the Purina checkerboards painted over.

Bernie Zamzow said, "We didn't quit Purina. Purina quit us."

Zamzows returned to making their own feed and never went back to Purina. It's better to make your own products and have control over them than to let others push you around. Doing so allows you to control the quality of the product and how it's sold.

Controlling Quality

Rick Zamzow believes one of the secrets to Zamzows' success lies in what his father always told Rick and Jim. "Pop used to say that you had to control the quality of your products from scratch to finish. So Jim and I have always come from a manufacturer's mindset. We'd buy a product from someone and it would sell and we'd say, 'We can do that but improve on it.' That's why we're still in the manufacturing business."

Rick with Iams pet food display

Zamzows has always been a stickler for product quality. Starting with co-founders August and Carmalita, every effort was made to manufacture and sell only the finest products. That especially applied to the very first Zamzows-brand feeds made at the Fairview store in 1933.

They used the University of Idaho's scientific formulas to make the feeds. Carmalita was the mixer and was very particular about how it was done. She'd put 100 pounds of grain on the floor in the back room of the Fairview store. Then she'd lay down another ingredient and another, until it looked like a layer cake. She'd rake it together until it was mixed perfectly. Then she'd load it into 100-pound bags and weigh them to make sure there was a little extra in each.

Grandma Z said she never remembered even *one* bag of Zamzows Feed coming back to the store because someone was not satisfied. Zamzows continued to use University of Idaho formulas to make their own feeds until they became a Purina dealer. Over the years, Zamzows pioneered many new products in the feed, pet, and lawn and garden industries.

Mentors Clay Mathile and Lester McCracken

Jim and Rick both learned a great deal about retail, developing their own products, and quality control from their mentors Clay Mathile and Lester McCracken.

When Rick Zamzow was just a 9th grader at West Junior High School in Boise, he did a school report on Union Farm and Garden. Even in 1964, Jim and Rick had dreams of someday going into the retail business. To complete his report, Rick visited Union Farm and Garden and conducted a face-to-face interview with the store's founder, the renowned lawn and garden expert, Lester McCraken.

Rick said, "Lester McCracken was one of our mentors. He has forgotten more about lawn and garden than most people will ever know. He was a great man. Little did he know by letting me interview him that day, he had just created his competitor for years down the road!"

Another mentor of Rick's was Clay Mathile, the CEO and owner of the Iams Company. While it was Paul Iams who founded the company, it was Clay Mathile who provided the vision to enable Iams to become a world leader in dog and cat nutrition. He also taught Rick Zamzow about premium pet foods.

"Clay Mathile was one of my greatest mentors. He had standards of quality. He was also an amazing realist and embodied the same type of business ethics that we had. 'Don't ever make it cheaper' was Clay's credo. Whereas other companies' attitude was typically 'How cheap can we make it?'"

Some manufacturers use something called *lowest-cost formulation*. In simple terms, this means the actual formulas of their pet foods can vary based on the cost of ingredients. If they can find a cheaper product that will work, even if it doesn't work as well, that's what they use, until they can find something even cheaper. The price the consumer pays for the product stays the same, or even goes up. Thus, the manufacturer wins with lowest-cost formulation, but the consumer, and ultimately the pet, loses.

Rick summed it up by saying, "It's the difference between someone who really cares about the animals and the culture of their company versus someone who only cares about the almighty buck."

Both mentors proved to be key influences on both Rick and Jim over the years. And for the most part, as long as Lester McCraken was running Union Farm and Garden, and Clay Mathile owned Iams, both companies were very successful. But leaders retire or turn their power over to younger managers who may forsake the principles and standards that made their companies successful in the first place.

Union Farm and Garden ended up going out of business in the late 1990s. The Iams Company brought in Harvard MBAs to manage the company and eventually sold out to Procter & Gamble. But the principles of these two great men are still alive and well at Zamzows, because Jim and Rick have never forgotten the many good things they learned from Lester McCracken and Clay Mathile.

Learning to Develop Brands

As Zamzows began to sell more Iams pet food, Iams made Zamzows one of its first distributors west of the Mississippi. Iams was a growing company and needed a strong distributor in Idaho and eastern Oregon. At first, all Zamzows wanted was the distributor discount. This worked for a while, but soon Iams demanded that Zamzows really get into the distribution business.

Jim and Rick opened up a few other outlets that were selling Iams. They got Iams into Forest Halls Hardware in Burley. They met with Dr. Marty Becker, a young veterinarian in Twin Falls, who tried Iams and liked it. He also liked the added revenue that selling a premium pet food brought to his practice. In fact, Dr. Becker liked it so much that he bought an entire truckload of another brand of pet food.

On their next visit, Jim and Rick asked him how it was selling. Dr. Becker said, "Very slowly." In fact, he now had a two-year supply. Rick educated Dr. Becker on how to cash-flow premium pet food. Dr. Becker took that knowledge and went on to become a national speaker, teaching other veterinarians how to make money selling premium pet foods. In fact, Marty Becker is now a best-selling author, educator, and even a media personality on ABC-TV's *Good Morning America*.

Left to right: Karen, Jim, Rick

Soon it became obvious to the Iams Company that these two Zamzow guys could effectively convince other retailers to take on the Iams line of premium pet food. But the Iams Company wanted Zamzows to separate their retail and wholesale divisions. Other retailers didn't want to openly buy Iams pet food from a competing retailer.

Rick Zamzow was getting bored. Needing a new challenge, he took over Iams distribution. They called the new division Wholesale Pet Food and Supplies.

Jim said, "This will be a big challenge for you."

IF YOU WANT TO DO IT RIGHT, MAKE IT YOURSELF

Beyond keeping the Iams Company happy, and the economic benefits of Zamzows getting paid for every bag of Iams pet food sold in Idaho and eastern Oregon, there was another important benefit: Zamzows learned how to develop brands.

Rick explained, "It was then we realized that we could develop brands of our own. We realized these manufacturers wanted us. That's when we developed Zamzows Professional brand pet foods, Save-a-Tree, Clean and Easy Cat Litter, and a host of other Zamzows brands."

Rick Zamzow with his dog, Katie

Rick credits the development of Zamzows' own brands to saving the company from the invasion of big box stores and national brands. "The reason why I and every other person at Zamzows still has a job is because of these proprietary products. Service is important and is part of the big picture, but I would say more than any other thing, what has kept us successful is the fact that we have our own lines."

Bernie added that brands are important as long as you have the service to go with them, and Jim pointed out that Zamzows brands were also better than the national brands they replaced.

The success of Zamzows products is the whole package: a superior product, great service, and complete control of the product's quality. If you've got all three, you've got a winner.

Just How Many Dogs Do You Feed?

The ultimate test in developing your own brand is how well it is accepted by the marketplace. August and Carmalita found immediate acceptance for their high quality ground grains and mixed feeds in the 1930s. Bernie Zamzow developed a full line of superior Zamzows-brand feeds after he gave Purina the boot in the mid-1960s. So it's been very rewarding for Jim and Rick to experience similar success with the animal feeds, pet foods, and lawn and garden products they have developed.

One Fourth of July weekend, Rick Zamzow found out firsthand just how popular Zamzows-brand dog foods had become. He was on the South Fork of the Salmon River and started talking to a husband and wife who were fishing. They chatted about fishing and they introduced themselves.

"I'm Rick Zamzow."

The woman said, "Oh, 'Zamzows' Zamzow? You feed my dogs! Do you want to see them?"

The couple opened up the truck and out came two beautiful yellow labs. She said, "I just love your dog food!"

One dog was on Grandma Z's dog food and the other was eating Zamzows Professional Senior formula. She knew all about the foods.

Farther down the river, Rick introduced himself to another man who replied, "Are you the 'Zamzows' Zamzow? I'm feeding my dog your dog food!"

Rick's friend Randy Hemmer, who was along for the fishing trip, turned to Rick and asked, "Just how much damn dog food do you sell, Zamzow?"

Zamzows sells an incredible amount of dog food—dozens of semi-trucks full each month, and growing. Developing their own brands has paid off. Their dedication to quality is a big part of what has made them successful.

7

Bigger Is Not Always Better

Zamzows Commandment of Good Business #7:

Grow your business only as fast as you can handle it. Bigger is not always better.

Too Many Horses

Jim was once asked to meet with a lady who was having trouble with her horses. The lady had about 100 horses and they just weren't doing well. They weren't reproducing or performing well and were showing classic signs of poor health and inadequate nutrition.

Jim asked a loaded question, "Does this lady have adequate finances and property to take care of 100 horses?"

The answer was a resounding no.

Jim then posed these questions: "Wouldn't it make sense for her to sell 90 of those horses and take care of 10? Feed the 10 animals properly, have time to groom them, get them shod, and train them? Wouldn't she then have time to get 10 healthy foals, and isn't it better to have 10 horses and 10 healthy foals than to have 100 sick horses with no prospect of foals?"

This lesson reflects the Zamzow family's belief about business as well. In the early 1970s, when Jim and Rick had just bought the company and were beginning to taste success, Jim was approached by a man who told him he could leverage his assets and borrow $10 million. That way, the man told Jim, he and Rick could build 10 new stores right away.

Jim agreed he probably *could* borrow $10 million and indeed *could* build 10 new stores. The man asked, "Why won't you do it?"

Jim replied rather emphatically, "Because I can't take care of the three stores I have now! When I learn how to take care of the three stores I have, then we'll put more in."

According to Jim, "We didn't have any master's degrees in business administration. We had the school of hard knocks. It's not how big you are. It's how good you are at taking care of the business you already have. I don't *want* to get any bigger if we can't take care of the business we already have."

Put a Tiger in Your Store

Over the years, members of the Zamzow family as well as Zamzows employees have had a lot of creative ideas, some of them better than others. One time Jim and Ken Kirkbride, a store manager, decided to bring a Bengal tiger into the Fairview store. They figured the tiger would generate lots of traffic. They were right, but both Zamzows and their customers got more than they bargained for.

Jim knew a gal who used to work for the animal act Siegfried and Roy in Las Vegas. One day she said, "Hey Jim, if you want to generate some traffic to your store, I've got a male Bengal tiger I can bring in for a day. You'll have more people than you can imagine."

When the tiger showed up, it was impressive. Zamzows ran an ad in the *Idaho Statesman* newspaper saying, "Come see our kitty."

Well, folks did. In fact, that tiger brought in so many people that many paying customers couldn't find a place to park and left. Most of the people who came to see the tiger didn't buy anything. They were only there to look. Additionally, there were so many people in the store that shoplifting increased.

But the topper was a lady in a beautiful silk dress who walked up to the tiger. She must have been wearing some kind of perfume because, as she stood there looking at him, that big cat turned around, lifted his tail, and sprayed her with urine, apparently attracted to her scent and simply doing what male cats do—marking her with his scent.

BIGGER IS NOT ALWAYS BETTER

Despite the massive amount of people the tiger drew to the store, Zamzows never considered bringing in a tiger again. It killed what would ordinarily have been the busiest day of the week and proved to be a major inconvenience for the customers.

Jim said, "We learned this lesson: no amount of traffic is worth it if it hurts your regular trade and keeps you from giving customers the service they deserve."

Visualize Using Your Turn Signal

While it's important to only take on what you can handle, that doesn't mean you shouldn't stretch and grow. The key is to have vision for where you're going and to communicate that vision to everyone involved. Jim Zamzow always wanted Zamzows to be the largest garden store in Idaho. In the late 1960s and early 1970s, that honor belonged to Union Farm and Garden. Jim felt that with a lot of work, Zamzows could someday become the largest garden store in the state.

"I don't think I knew anything about goal-setting at the time, but what I wanted was to be bigger than Union Farm and Garden." So Jim subtly began changing the way Zamzows did things. He started stocking different lawn and garden merchandise, put more emphasis on bulk items, and brought in some of the same or comparable products that Union Farm and Garden carried.

Garden products outside storefront at Meridian Mill

One day, Rick confronted Jim and asked him, "What are you trying to do here? Why are you doing this?"

So Jim told him, "I want Zamzows to be the biggest garden store in the state of Idaho!"

Rick looked back at him in surprise and yelled, "Well, why didn't you say so?"

At that moment, according to Jim, he caught the vision. Rick has said that every company must communicate the company's vision and purpose "all the way down to where the rubber hits the road." In other words, everyone from the owners of the company all the way down to the most junior employee must be aware of the company's overall mission. Having the same vision aligns everyone to the goal so they can work together to achieve success.

Refocusing the Business

In the late 1980s Zamzows' focus changed. The company had moved into their new corporate offices at Glenwood and Chinden. Jim Zamzow had moved his office there and Ken Kirkbride was now the general manager of the five retail stores. Rick Zamzow was running Wholesale Pet, distributor of Iams pet foods for all of southern Idaho, eastern Oregon, and Utah. The Iams Company wanted Zamzows to open a second distribution center in Salt Lake City, Utah. Rick hired a general manager for Wholesale Pet and a manager for the Salt Lake facility, and he hit the road again as a super-salesman, opening up new retail and veterinarian accounts. Things were going great in the distribution business. Meanwhile, Jim was building an organic lawn service company.

However, the retail business began to get off track. Zamzows began advertising discounts in an effort to compete. They hired Alan Toennis to run Wholesale Pet, which freed resources up to take a good look at the business as a whole and better define the Zamzows brand.

When Rick attended the Iams strategic planning session, he realized that as a company, Zamzows didn't know who they were. He brought in a guy from Sun Valley named Craig Phelan who helped Rick with strategic planning. They looked at the business and asked what its strengths, weaknesses, and opportunities were. Every employee filled out a survey based on those points.

BIGGER IS NOT ALWAYS BETTER

After looking at all those surveys, it was confirmed: Zamzows didn't know who they were. They didn't know who their customers were and their customers didn't know who they were or what they stood for.

Rick working at the first Emmett store

Rick said, "What we had to do first was determine who we were, what we stood for, and who we wanted our customer to be. Then we started looking at the product mix and it didn't fit. Discounting all the time didn't fit our strategy either."

So Zamzows hired Art Gregory as marketing and communications director. At the time, Art was the station manager for the Boise radio station KHEZ-FM.

At the first lunch meeting with Art, Rick said, "Art, we're doing all this cutesy stuff on the radio but we don't know who we are and we don't have a consistent plan."

Rick realized Zamzows wasn't focused on retail, which was what Zamzows was to the consumer. Zamzows was not capitalizing on their unique research and manufacturing abilities.

THAT REMINDS ME OF A STORY

Another important accomplishment came out of the strategic planning: the company mission statement. It's called the Zamzows Way: "*To provide the highest quality, environmentally-sound products at a service level beyond our customers' expectations.*"

Rick said, "We reasoned we better get our bases covered because the big box stores were coming to town. We'd better know who we are, what we do, and what we stand for. That's how our mission statement evolved."

From that point on, they decided to focus on pets, pet-related items, and lawn and garden. They started focusing on their own proprietary products.

Even with all of this determination, it took a long time to get all Zamzows employees on board. Old habits are hard to break, plus changing strategies takes time. It's like turning a jet airplane around on the runway. You don't do it instantly. A lot of people didn't agree with the direction the company needed to go. But this change in direction was one of the key factors to Zamzows' survival against the big box stores. It's vital to know who you are and what you stand for, and to get everyone in the company on board with that mission.

If you don't have values, you have nothing. You have to stand for something. Everybody's got a mission statement, but it's important to live up to that mission statement. A mission isn't just words—it is actions.

Art Gregory with Grandma Z

8

There's Nothing Like Money in the Bank

Zamzows Commandment of Good Business #8:

Avoid borrowing money; but if you have to, pay it back quickly.

Avoid Borrowing

The Zamzow family has never been keen on borrowing money. Both August and Bernie believed borrowing was a necessary evil, something to do only as a last resort.

If August owed any money, he wouldn't be happy until he repaid it. When the family lived in Meridian, they had a neighbor they'd trade work with. August owed more hours than what he was able to repay and it bothered him until he could either pay it or work it off. He didn't like to be indebted to anyone.

Bernie borrowed money to build the new Fairview store, although he didn't want to. Jim and Rick borrowed a great deal of money for their expansion of Zamzows but, just like their grandfather and their dad, they have always paid it back quickly.

Bernie pointed out that things have changed a lot over the generations. He remembers working all day long, 10 full hours, for only a dollar. He took any work he could get in high school, mostly farm labor and hard manual labor like loading, bucking, stacking hay, and thrashing grain.

One time Bernie helped a poor, old farmer on one whole hay crop. When he finished the farmer just said, "All I've got is hay and I can't even sell it. But you can have hay to pay for the work you did." So Bernie took hay as payment and used it to feed the cows.

He worked for the farmer a couple of summers with August's team and equipment. They were glad to be able to work and take the pay in hay because they couldn't raise enough on their farm to last the entire year. "We didn't think anything about it," said Bernie. "That's just the way you existed in those days."

Bernie knew the value of trading rather than borrowing when you don't have the money you need. It's a lesson that many people today have forgotten, but it's a great way to stay out of debt. Take what you can get and don't live above your means, and you'll be able to rise out of your financial struggles much faster without debt to drag you back down.

August Zamzow in his garden

The Money in the Prince Albert Cans

Bernie Zamzow planned to be an educated farmer and had won a scholarship to the University of Idaho from the Union Pacific Railroad as the Ada County agricultural student attaining the highest rating in their annual competition. He was also one of the leaders of the Boise High School FFA (Future Farmers of America) chapter and a newspaper carrier with the *Idaho Statesman*.

"We learned to be very thrifty. My dad told me if I made a dollar here or a nickel there, never spend it all. If you can only save one penny from every dollar, you'll never be broke. A penny wouldn't amount to much today, but it was good sum of money to us kids then."

When he was in high school, Bernie had a friend who ran a paper route. When he got another job and decided to let his paper route go, Bernie grabbed it! He made a dollar a day. He would go into a little confectionary store across the street from the high school, look at the nickel candy bars, and decide he'd worked too hard for that nickel to buy a candy bar.

The dollar Bernie made each day from his paper route was saved in a rather unconventional manner. It was the early 1930s, the heart of the Great Depression. His bank was August's empty Prince Albert Pipe Tobacco cans. He'd fold the dollar bills and put them in the cans.

In their old barn there was a loose rock that he could move to hide his Prince Albert cans. Then, when his sister Margaret got appendicitis, gangrene set in and she nearly died. She was in the hospital about a month, and when it came time to pay the bill, Carmalita and August didn't have enough money. So Bernie got out his Prince Albert cans and gave them the money—$270.

The money from his paper route was supposed to be Bernie's college fund. That money now gone, Bernie hitchhiked up Idaho Highway 55 to attend the University of Idaho where he immediately got a job. He thought nothing of the contribution he'd just made to his family. "Being on a farm, we always had work to do. And we learned to work at a young age. There were always chores to do and cows to milk. As a young man, I'd help Dad harvest and put in the crop. At the time, we did everything by horse and wagon and didn't have any motorized equipment. We normally had from 15 to 20 head of cows to milk twice a day. Everyone pitched in and it was just the normal way of living. Everything went into the same pot."

You can always work to earn more money, but family is priceless. Bernie valued his family and knew better than to be stingy. His attitude of generosity carried into the way he ran the Zamzows business, always giving customers more than they paid for.

Proceed With Caution—Buying the Store

Fear of failure has always been a reason for slow, modest growth at Zamzows. When August Zamzow bought the bankrupt Snodgrass Mill, he gave the family farm back to the bank so he wouldn't overextend himself. When Jim and Rick bought Zamzows from their dad, they were also afraid they would fail.

Groundbreaking with four generations of Zamzows:
Grandma Z, Bernie, Jim, Jos, and Callie

THERE'S NOTHING LIKE MONEY IN THE BANK

The first year the new Fairview store was in operation, there was a lot of tension in the family. The conservative nature of Bernie Zamzow and his aversion to borrowing money was something Jim and Rick felt looming over them all the time.

Rick said, "When we first built the retail store, Jim and I didn't know what to do. We were just scared to death of failure. Pop was always adamant about teaching us to work and we didn't have a lot of money to throw away. There was no cushion."

Both Jim and Rick had other career opportunities besides working for their dad. In high school, Jim had the chance to work for a local farmer who offered to give him the farm if he'd work for him several years. The farmer apparently liked Jim and had no children who wanted to take over his farm. Jim was very flattered by the offer and thought about it for a time, but decided to attend Boise Junior College (BJC) instead.

Bernie had always encouraged both of his boys to work elsewhere. That way they would gain other work experience. Jim worked at Brass Lamp Pizza, and Rick fought fires during the summer and worked for several retail stores such as Buttrey Foods.

After Jim finished two years at BJC, he enlisted in the Air National Guard. In 1967, the Vietnam War was drafting every young man in sight. Jim decided to enlist in the reserve in the hope of not having to go to Vietnam. When he was sent to Basic Training at Lackland Airforce Base in San Antonio, Texas, Jim saw the ravages of war firsthand. He knew if Rick were drafted and sent to Vietnam, he might end up in body bag like the hundreds of men he saw coming back. He called Rick and told him to enlist in Air National Guard immediately. Rick took his advice and did his stint right out of high school.

When he finished college, Jim got an offer to go to work for J.J. Newberry stores in Minneapolis. Jim visited with his counselor who pointed out that, if he ever did want to take over Zamzows, he needed to learn the business while his father was still there to teach him. So Jim went to work for his dad at Zamzows.

THAT REMINDS ME OF A STORY

Meanwhile, when he returned from his Air National Guard Basic Training, Rick attended the University of Idaho for one semester. But Rick was, in his own words, "never cut out to be a Vandal." Returning to Boise, he enrolled at BSU, which was then called Boise State College. He then joined Jim at Zamzows, working 30 hours a week while going to Boise State as a full-time student.

In 1970, Jim and Rick finally talked their dad into building the new Fairview store. The Boise valley was growing. Fairview Avenue between Curtis Road and Cole was the new center of commerce in Boise and Zamzows was located right in the middle of it.

Their dad asked them, "Why should I risk my retirement money on a new store?"

They replied, "Because it's a good investment, that's why."

They finally got their wish. Bernie borrowed $125,000 and built a brand-new store at Fairview and Liberty, just behind the old Zamzows store. Jim and Rick both worked there, knowing they would someday have the opportunity to buy the company. But they were kept in the dark by their dad, who wouldn't show them the books. The brothers always thought they were going broke.

What Bernie did show them was how much they had to sell to make the payment to the bank, and if they missed just one payment, he'd shut the store down and sell it to someone else.

The first year the new store was open was 1971. Jim and Rick did okay with sales. But as the Fairview area grew, so did Zamzows. Jim and Rick got into the lawn and garden business in a big way. Sales doubled every year. Jim and Rick kept asking their dad to sell them the store. The $125,000 loan was paid off early and, in 1973, Jim and Rick talked Bernie into adding onto the store.

Sales doubled again but Jim and Rick still didn't own the store. By 1978, Zamzows was doing so much business the boys tried to force the issue: "When are you going to sell us the business? If you don't do it now, we'll never be able to afford it at the rate we're growing."

This time, Bernie finally said, "All right."

THERE'S NOTHING LIKE MONEY IN THE BANK

Shortly after selling the company to Jim and Rick in 1978, Bernie had a mild heart attack. Rick joked that selling the store to them may have been what caused his dad's heart attack. But Bernie said, "I had the heart attack after we'd completed the contract. I think it was purely coincidental. I hadn't had any problems healthwise and that wasn't the reason I sold. No, I figured it was time for them to take over. I had no thoughts of quitting, however. I just thought it was time for them to take it over. That's how Stan and I had worked it with my folks."

Zamzows store in Emmett

Rick said Bernie financed the purchase. The price he and Jim paid was based on the worth of the physical assets. There was, however, interest involved and the brothers paid their dad a tidy sum each month for many years.

Sales and markets continued to expand under Jim and Rick's ownership over the next few years. A fourth location in Emmett was opened, the Meridian retail store was remodeled, the Kuna store rebuilt, and the Fairview store was expanded again. In every case, they proceeded with caution. Zamzows still expands, but not without careful consideration of how much it's going to cost and what could happen if something goes wrong. If the risk looks too great, they wait. Whether you're building a store or entering a busy intersection, it's best to look both ways and proceed with caution.

Jim Zamzow says people assume it's easy to start a business. Some folks think he and Rick simply walked into a successful business that was given to them by their dad. Nothing could be further from the truth. Working that closely with family members day after day in a family business can take its toll.

Jim said, "I don't think the average person realizes what goes into the development of a business. The *dynamics* of the family certainly come into play. Take someone with a mind like me: structured and scientific. Rick's mind is more administrative. Then, factor in both of us being of equal vote and neither one of us seeming to agree, and you may get a sense of how difficult it can be. Still, there are advantages. Each one of us keeps the other in check. Rick's conservativism has always kept me in line. I would have probably been planning our first trip to the moon somewhere around 1975 if it weren't for Rick."

It's important to have balance in your approach. Jim and Rick made a good team with their varied skills and viewpoints, and together, they expanded Zamzows significantly.

I'll Throw in the Rusty Engines for Free

In the late 1980s, Jim Zamzow was looking for a site for a new Zamzows Distribution Center. At that time, Zamzows had five stores: two in Boise and three small stores in Meridian, Kuna, and Emmett. Jim and Rick both wanted to add more stores but needed to expand the company's distribution center before they could do so. Located right between the company's two biggest stores was a former construction office that also had a large warehouse, which could be expanded, and enough land to build a second warehouse. Best of all, the price was right.

But it was full of junk: old rusty engines, steel pipes, and literally tons of old concrete. The bank that owned the property knew they had a lemon on their hands. The property had been condemned and even the sign advertising it for sale was falling down.

Jim called the bank and asked what they wanted for the property. The price was around $77,000. Jim checked on what it would take to remove the scrap metal and the concrete. He thought the scrap metal could be removed by a salvage guy he knew. Jim asked him how much he'd give him for all that metal. It turned out to be worth a couple thousand dollars. The concrete could be removed by a demolition company Jim had worked with in the past. So Jim called the bank back and offered them 50 percent of the asking price.

The bank accepted the offer if he'd take the property as is. Jim was able to clean the place up and even found over 1,000 pounds of aluminum tubing, which he took right next door to Boise Recycling and sold for a good price!

That small investment appreciated rapidly, thanks to the small purchase price and some substantial improvements to the property. As soon as the land and buildings were cleaned up, Jim moved Zamzows' corporate offices there and added on to the large garage, turning it into a very nice warehouse and distribution center for Iams pet foods. A short time later, a larger warehouse was also built on the site, allowing Zamzows to expand by building two new retail stores. Eventually, Zamzows retail stores were doing so much business that both the original and the new warehouse were no longer big enough to handle the company's sales, and Zamzows moved to a beautiful office and distribution center in Nampa.

Jim's resourcefulness and willingness to take on something no one else wanted to handle gave him an advantage that worked to great benefit for the Zamzows business. He was willing to do the work and research necessary and made a profit off a property that seemed more trouble than it was worth.

9

Employees Make Your Business

> **Zamzows Commandment of Good Business #9:**
>
> Employees make your company; seek out and hire good ones, train them, learn from them, and then do what's necessary to retain them.

Holy Kadiddlehopper! It's Les Tinkham

Zamzows has had many fantastic employees, some of them so close they were like family. A few in particular stand out for their impact on the business, including Les Tinkham and Walter Shepherd. These people have become important characters in the history of the Zamzows company.

Lester Tinkham worked for Zamzows from 1950 to 1972. He really hated swearing, so when he hit his finger with a hammer, Lester exclaimed, "Holy Kadiddlehopper!" Soon Les Tinkham was known to insiders at Zamzows Inc. as "Holy Kadiddlehopper."

Les Tinkham was an amazing worker who used old-fashioned common sense to conserve company resources. Maybe that's why Bernie Zamzow wanted to hire him so badly. Les Tinkham worked for the Perkins Store on the corner of Franklin and Cole. Bernie tried to hire Les many times. But Les said he couldn't quit working for Katherine and Harry, who had bought the Perkins store for him to run.

One day Bernie got a phone call from Les. "I think they're going to sell this store." He wondered if the offer Bernie made a while back was still available.

THAT REMINDS ME OF A STORY

"Yes, it certainly is."

Les Tinkham and Walt Shepherd taught Jim and Rick many valuable things. Jim said, "Pop taught us how to work at home, but when we were working at the mill, Walt's the one who taught us to work out there, and, when we were working at the Fairview store, Les Tinkham was our tutor."

Les Tinkham working in old Fairview store

Les taught Jim and Rick how to deliver coal. Jim said, "Les taught us how to properly put down a tarp so we caught every piece of coal. Then we'd pull down the tailgate and shovel it in. When we were done, you'd never know we'd even been there. We swept up afterward and always left the place cleaner than when we got there."

Les was so fiscally conservative he saved the cardboard placed between salt blocks and cut it up to make note pads. No printed note pads were ever purchased during the "old days" at Zamzows. Les Tinkham made them.

Jim said, "All the things I used to resent about Les Tinkham I now hold in high regard. Things like being conservative, how to save a bale of hay, how to quickly salvage a bag of feed that had just a hole poked in it before you lost the value of the bag."

In a way, Jim owes his first job as manager of the Fairview store to Les Tinkham. After the new Fairview store was constructed in 1970, Les asked to be transferred to run the new feed warehouse. Someone was needed to run the retail portion of the new store and Jim was called into the office by his dad and Walt Shepherd.

They asked Jim whether he'd consider being manager of the new store. If not, they'd have to go outside the company to hire someone. At the time, Jim knew nothing about it, but he said yes and took over as manager of the Fairview store in 1970. Les Tinkham became warehouse manager and finally resigned when the store got too big for his ability. Les Tinkham's name still comes up with fondness.

Walter Shepherd

Walt Shepherd taught Jim Zamzow to hammer a nail by telling him, "Get your butt behind you." Walt could pound a spike into a piece of wood in just a few seconds. There weren't many things Walt Shepherd couldn't do.

Bernie said, "He was a hard worker! Walt Shepherd was a Seabee in the service and when he came back, his family lived very close to the Fairview store. He had cows and chickens there and he rented land to farm. Besides that, he was an expert finish carpenter. I said anyone who'll work like that, if I could hire him, would be a real asset! I'd have three or four guys in one!"

Walt and Bernie became friends and Bernie would sell him feed for his livestock. He kept trying to get him to work for Zamzows but he'd always say, "No, I'm a carpenter and finish man, and you can't pay me enough." Plus, he liked what he was doing.

Bernie replied, "Yeah, but every morning you have to drive all the way to Nampa and back and it takes you an hour each way." He finally broke down and agreed to come to work for Zamzows.

Walt started with Bernie in the early 1950s when Zamzows opened the first Eagle store. When the new Meridian Mill opened, Walt Shepherd made all the display cases by hand. When Bernie decided to expand the mill and add on to it, Walt supervised the construction. And, when they built the new Fairview store, guess who supervised that? He ran the Meridian Mill for Bernie.

Rick says Walt Shepherd was strict with him and Jim when they worked at the mill. "I wanted to work *anywhere* in the company but under Walter!"

Walt Shepherd stayed with Zamzows for almost 30 years. He retired shortly before Jim and Rick made the final purchase of the store. His contribution to the company can't be overestimated.

Bernie, Jim, and Rick still have the highest regard for Les Tinkham and Walt Shepherd. Bernie explains, "They were as close to being family as you could hire. In other words, they were just as active and concerned with the business as we were."

In addition to Les Tinkham and Walt Shepherd, some of the other names of great employees include Bill Barkell, Dean Price, Max Badesheim, Georgie Titus, Eric Tabb, Bill Precht, Debbie Carrell, Stacy Boston, Tim Humphreys, and Ken Kirkbride. There are hundreds more who deserve mentioning, but rest assured that if someone stays with Zamzows for any length of time, they're a good employee.

Bernie's key employees were often treated more like friends than employees. Every Christmas and New Year's, Bernie always invited his key employees to come to the Fairview store and go down in the basement, play cards, drink whiskey, and smoke cigars. It was a tradition, and Bernie always enjoyed himself.

Bernie summed it all up in a short but profound statement that every employer in America should heed: "Employees make your company."

Sharing the Profits

In the early 1960s, Bernie Zamzow did something extraordinary for his employees. He started a retirement and a profit-sharing plan. A substantial percentage of each employee's pay was put aside for them in a special fund. It was over and above the employee's regular pay. Zamzows even pays 100 percent of the cost of administering the funds. When the employee is ready to retire, he or she should have a substantial amount—often over six figures—for retirement.

In addition to a retirement plan, the company has added a 401(k) plan where they match up to six percent of the employee's salary. There's also a yearly cash bonus awarded to full-time employees based on the profitability of the company. All together, employees can save almost 30 percent of their annual pay tax-free. Plus, the employee only contributes a small portion to just one of the plans. Zamzows pays the rest. After six years, the employee is fully "vested" in the plan, and 100 percent of the money is available to them upon leaving Zamzows.

Art speaking at groundbreaking event of Federal Way store in 1992

There is a good reason for rewarding employees well so they stay with the company. According to Bernie, good employees are the main reason for Zamzows' success. "Our family didn't do it ourselves. The employees did. It's loyal and aggressive employees who carry on the goals of the leaders and have made the difference."

Zamzows started that employee retirement fund when the government made it available. It has helped to generate good relationships with employees. Bernie and Stanley felt that by having this program, the employee would feel like he or she was part of the company and had a monetary interest in it. They wanted employees to have something they could look forward to and know that when they are old enough and feel like retiring, they will have some money to depend on.

Zamzows' retirement program has worked very well for most employees. Since the program was started in the early 1960s, there haven't been many years Zamzows *hasn't* put money in their employee retirement fund, which Bernie thinks is a good banner for the company. Carmalita and August always encouraged Bernie to save a little bit of every dollar for the future. With compound interest, even saving a little money each year can result in a fairly substantial sum when you want to retire. Bernie said, "Even if you don't have much, save a little every year. Those dollars will help you take care of yourself if you don't spend them."

The Surprise Trip to Costco

In 1996, Zamzows had a lackluster lawn and garden season. Rick Zamzow, company president at the time, was concerned. Sales were starting to soften after an economic boom. At the same time, employees were jumping ship for better-paying jobs at Micron, Hewlett-Packard, and other high-tech businesses. Rick came up with a radical idea—let your employees know you appreciate them by rewarding them in advance!

All Zamzows employees were informed they must attend a mandatory meeting at the company warehouse. Meetings would take place over a two-day period with half the staff attending one day and the rest of the staff the second day. At the start of the meeting, the staff were informed that they'd be leaving soon to "shop the competition." The staff was then told to get into several vans to be taken to PetSmart on Franklin Road in Boise. Once there, they would be told what to do next.

When the vans arrived at PetSmart, they drove behind the store and parked right next to Costco. The staff was beginning to wonder what was going on. They were told, "You'll see when we get there."

Once out of the vans, the staff was herded to the front door of Costco where Ken Kirkbride, Zamzows' general manager, was posted. As the staff entered Costco, they were each handed two $100 bills. The rules were simple: They were to go into Costco and buy *anything* they wanted for themselves. They were to spend *all* of the $200. Anything left would be collected at the door on the way out and would go back to Zamzows. And, finally, they only had one hour, so they'd better get going.

By the time the hour was up every Zamzows employee had a different attitude. It was quite a sight seeing them push baskets down the aisles of Costco trying to decide what to buy. Some had their carts piled high. Others carefully hand-picked one or two expensive items and then headed for the checkout lane.

The employees congregated at the store's front entrance and compared notes on what they'd just bought. There was a new spirit of camaraderie as employees who really didn't know each another very well got a glimpse of what their coworkers liked. Some dreams came true that day.

Before getting back into the vans, the employees were told, "Thank you. We appreciate having you as an employee and just wanted to do something nice for you and your family."

The second day, John Miller of Boise Television station KTVB showed up and filmed the final wave of Zamzows employees while they did their shopping. What Miller caught were happy Zamzows employees. At the end of his report he quipped, "Maybe *I'll* apply there!"

THAT REMINDS ME OF A STORY

It was difficult for the first wave of Zamzows employees to keep quiet about what happened. Yet somehow they did, and the second wave of employees was just as surprised as the first.

Zamzows pulled this employee surprise just once. It was deemed a huge success and the company had an excellent spring lawn and garden season and retained more employees that year. More importantly, the surprise trip to Costco shook things up and gave everyone in the company a new attitude and something to talk about. For everyone who was there, it's something no one will forget.

Zamzows knows the value of their employees—without the employees, there would be no business. They are the people who make the whole thing run and who provide the customer service Zamzows takes so much pride in. Once you've hired good employees, it's worth making an effort to keep them. A loyal employee is one of the greatest assets to a business.

10

A Good Steward to the Community Earth

Zamzows Commandment of Good Business #10:

Be a good steward of the earth's resources and all living things on it. We're all part of one big community.

We'd Rather Lose the Business

Jim Zamzow was faced with a hard decision to either sell Zamzows manufactured feeds with the harmful chemical urea in them and remain competitively priced, or take it out and risk losing virtually all the company's dairy feed business. Jim chose to take the urea out and for good reason.

Urea is a nonprotein form of nitrogen. It's an artificial protein. It allows feed companies to say "14 percent protein" on the feed bag when, truthfully, there may only be 10 percent that's natural. The other 4 percent is artificial protein, which practically costs nothing but is harmful to cattle.

Zamzows Dairy Feed was 14 percent all-natural protein and all their competitors were using 4 percent urea to boost their protein. They could sell feed for a dollar less per 80 pounds. Jim knew that, in time, feeds with urea would cause urea poisoning, nitrogen poisoning, and kidney problems for the cows. On behalf of the farmer, Jim chose not to use it. Plus, any cross-contamination from dairy feed to horse feed could cause kidney failure in horses: a single-stomach animal cannot deal with urea in their feed.

A Zamzows employee said, "Jim, we've got to go back to urea or we're going to lose all of our dairy business."

Jim said, "Dave, I'd rather lose all of our dairy business than do the wrong thing for the customer."

As a consequence, Zamzows lost all of their dairy business because their price was higher than urea-based products. Jim says, "It may not have been a good business decision but it was a good ethical decision. At least I know I did the right thing by the customer."

Zamzows believes it's important to be a good steward of the earth's resources and all living things on it. We're all part of one big community.

Carmalita's garden behind the house on Fairview

You Stay Out of My Garden!

Jim first began to question the schooling he'd received that taught him to use chemicals on plants when he visited Grandma Z's garden one day. Grandma Z always raised an incredible garden. After he got out of college, Jim paid her a visit and offered his newfound expertise.

He said, "Grandma, we could really help your garden a lot. We ought to put about 10 pounds of 16-16-16 on it." It was a combination of nitrogen, phosphorus, and potassium. He continued, "If we throw some of that on your garden it'll really make it grow!"

Grandma Z put her hands up and said, "*You stay out of my garden!*"

Jim felt a little put out. He didn't understand. After all, he'd been through fertilizer classes. After he regained his composure, Jim asked Grandma Z, "Why?"

She explained that August saved all the manure from their poultry and dairy cattle, which he piled up, turned, and then spread on their farm land. They raised all their own corn and hay to feed to their animals. Natural manure was the only fertilizer they'd used since it was all they could afford.

She then showed Jim a picture of Grandpa Zamzow standing on a hay derrick holding his shovel high in the air, with the corn as high as the shovel. That was the size and quality of corn they always grew. They never had any corn earworm, corn borer, corn smut, or any of the other insects and diseases that seemed to plague other farmers.

The other farmers all applied chemical fertilizer, which made their corn grow very rapidly for several years. Then, they all were plagued by insects and diseases. She always suspected it had something to do with the use of chemical fertilizers. That was when Jim began to understand how important it is to take care of the earth in order to get the best results from it.

My Lawn Looks Lousy

Jim had a favorite customer at the Fairview store in the early 1970s. He was a Scotts lawn products customer. Everything he used was Scotts. He'd been doing this for about three or four years and he came to Jim one Saturday and said, "Jim, I want you to come look at my lawn."

"I really don't have time," said Jim.

THAT REMINDS ME OF A STORY

Jim in garden with pumpkin

"But I'm just flabbergasted. Please come look at it and see if you can tell me what's going on with it."

Jim drove over there and the man's lawn was riddled with disease. It had every disease Jim could diagnose, along with insects galore. Further investigation uncovered the fact that the neighbor, whose lawn looked pretty good, only applied natural steer manure once each year.

The customer asked why the neighbor's lawn looked better and Jim said, "When these disease spores blow over from your lawn, his lawn will also get sick and, when insects hatch and move over, his lawn will get them, too."

The customer said, "I don't buy it. Dogs run across it. Kids run across it. These lawns have been growing together for the longest time and all he does is put on cow manure once a year. His lawn is doing better than mine and I want to know why."

Jim suggested applications of Scotts disease control and insect control.

He said, "Jim, I've put everything on my lawn you told me to and I still have these problems. Why?"

Jim displaying handful of radishes

Jim didn't know why. So he sent a sample of the customer's lawn to the experts at Scotts research division, maker of the chemical fertilizers and pesticides the customer was applying. The answer Jim got from Scotts was to apply *more* Scotts chemical fertilizers, pesticides, and fungicides.

Jim rejected that answer and consulted more experts at Michigan State, Cornell, and Penn State Universities. All of them gave him the same answer.

Jim reflected on the experience: "I went through a year or so knowing there was more to the story than what the big chemical companies were telling us, but I didn't know what it was."

There is an old Buddhist proverb that says, *When the student is ready, the teacher will appear.* Jim's teacher appeared when his accountant told him there was a man he might want to talk to. This man was a soil expert and was able to solve the disease problems of the Collier family's citrus groves in Florida that no chemical company could. His name was C.J. Fenzau. Jim set up a meeting to talk with him at a coffee shop.

Jim and C.J. sat together for hours over coffee. He could answer every question Jim had. C.J. had been trained to use chemical products by Midwestern land grant universities, but through experience he learned that nature has her own way of doing things and that man can't circumvent what nature has to offer.

This was when Jim first learned the basic concepts of soil health: the most important ingredient of good soil is humus.

C.J. said, "What you're doing in your lawns is a very basic thing. I've seen it happen on every farm in this country and this is what I've spent the last 20 years of my career trying to correct. The health of your soil is the health of your plants."

Healthy soil requires 12-20 parts carbon to 1 part nitrogen, with the ideal ratio being 20-1. The earth naturally balances itself through the decomposition of leaves and other plant materials. Unfortunately, man is not content to let Mother Nature run the earth, resulting in the basic problem of *soil imbalance*.

C.J. said, "Every time we put on one unit of nitrogen, bacteria in the soil will burn up 20 units of carbon (the organic matter which is humus). So every time you apply nitrogen, you burn up humus."

Thus, every time a chemical company applies nitrogen through chemical fertilizer, they're burning up the humus in the soil. When that happens, a chain reaction is started that may take up to three years to completely manifest in the form of a crop failure.

The humus is what the bacteria live on, as well as the fungi, the yeast, and all the other microbes. They feed on the carbon material—the dead leaves and so on. Then they secrete a sticky substance that holds water. It also causes the soil to flocculate so that water can drain through, the soil can hold water, air can circulate in the soil, and the soil can create a healthy root system for a plant.

Those bacteria and fungi excrete antibiotic chemicals that protect them from other organisms. These substances also protect the plant from diseases. A stressed plant is more susceptible to insects and disease. Soil is a living organism, containing beneficial microscopic plants and microbes. Never apply anything that will harm them.

C.J. Fenzau also brought to light the notion that insects and disease are nature's garbage collectors. Jim says, "They remove plants that are not fit for human or animal consumption and indicate an imbalance in the soil."

Trace minerals are also important. When you don't have adequate humus, you don't have adequate biological activity. When that happens, it means you don't have adequate trace mineral release from the soil. If the soil has been harvested for some time, trace minerals may not be present in adequate amounts.

When you mow your lawn, you are essentially harvesting a crop. The crop is the grass you cut each week and throw away. A better approach is to grind up or "mulch" the clippings into the lawn and leave them there for fertilizer. That way, you are not removing all the trace minerals and nutrients from the soil and failing to replace them with more.

As a result of that one meeting, Jim Zamzow began to invent organic-based products to solve lawn problems by giving the soil what it needs to prevent disease and insects and produce healthy plants.

The Story of Save-a-Tree

Jim Zamzow's first big break in the development of the product Save-a-Tree (now called Thrive) came when he discovered humic acid. Humic acid was economical, easy to apply, and supplied essential humus in a concentrated form. Jim took his new discovery and soon developed Zamzows Prescription Treatment, a liquid fertilizer that could be applied to the foliage of house plants, yielding spectacular results. That led to the development of Zamzows organic-based Lawn Food in 1988. Jim tested it against all major national brands and perfected a formula that worked better than any of them.

In 1993, Jim developed Zamzows All Natural Flower and Garden Food, an organic-based fertilizer for gardens and flowerbeds that also worked better than any other garden fertilizer. The following year, he developed Zamzows Recharger Fall and Winter Lawn Fertilizer and field-tested it with similar positive results. But the ultimate product was yet to come.

In 1997, he introduced the revolutionary product Save-a-Tree. Finally, here was a product in a concentrated liquid form that combined what Jim had learned over the past 30 years. It incorporated everything he knew about soil health and plant fertility and how to stimulate biological activity. It was safe, nontoxic, and contained every trace mineral in the periodic table.

Save-a-Tree was first made in small batches and given to a few of Jim's friends and customers who had a problematic tree or plant. The results were so stunning and so spectacular that almost everyone who tried the product wanted more. Jim made a large batch and had his son, Josua, test it at the Meridian Zamzows store. Jos was manager there at the time and the customers who tried it wanted more.

Soon, demand for Save-a-Tree exceeded Jim's production capabilities. He and Jos went shopping for a liquid fertilizer manufacturing plant. They found one in a distant city and had it disassembled and moved to Nampa.

Sales of Save-a-Tree began to take off. In April of 2000, Jim Zamzow announced Project Tree 2000 and offered to donate up to a million dollars' worth of Save-a-Tree to the state of Idaho and every city and county within Zamzows' trade area.

The Idaho State Parks Department, Boise City, the City of Meridian, and the Idaho Botanical Garden all took him up on his offer, and Zamzows provided enough product, free of charge, to treat every tree owned by the City of Boise, the City of Meridian, Bruneau Canyon State Park, and the Idaho Botanical Garden.

Most of the cities and parks noted have become regular users of Save-a-Tree. In fact, Save-a-Tree is sold by the tanker-truck load to Skagit Valley Bulbs, the Northwest's largest grower of tulip bulbs, located in Mount Vernon, Washington.

In 1999, Jim invented a companion product to Save-a-Tree. It was a granular humus product called Zamzows Huma-Green, made to help lawns and gardens cope with the stress of summer heat. By adding natural iron and humus to the soil, Huma-Green reduced water consumption and allowed lawns and gardens to flourish in the heat of summer while not causing excessive growth. Save-a-Tree added to Huma-Green was like magic and both products seemed to work together much better and much quicker than they did alone.

By 2001, Zamzows was offering a full collection of environmentally-sound products for lawns and gardens, all designed especially for Treasure Valley soils. That same year, Zamzows introduced the Grandma Z's line of all-natural products, including all-natural compost and potting soil. Grandma Z's potting soil contains mycorrhizae, a fungus that opens up the soil, allowing it to take in air, water, and nutrients. Mycorrhizae is also the key ingredient in Save-a-Tree Plus, another liquid soil-enhancer product introduced in 2002.

Mother Nature is clearly in control of all of the Zamzows environmentally-sound products, something both Grandma Z and C.J. Fenzau would approve of. Now more than ever, there is a crying need for Thrive and other environmentally-safe products.

Jim says, "If man were dead and gone from this earth for 50 years, Mother Nature would have it right back to the way it was supposed to be. It's just that we continually and continuously pollute. It is all nature can do to keep up with us. If you have a toxic waste spill, pay attention to how nature does it. Nature starts on the edge and starts its biological process of decomposing."

That is exactly what Save-a-Tree/Thrive does. It works *with* Mother Nature to stimulate natural organic activity in the soil, feeding and encouraging the microbes and other living creatures to do their jobs.

In the mid-2000s, Zamzows renamed Save-a-Tree "Thrive" to broaden the product's appeal and let the public know it would work well on everything that grows rather than just trees. In the spring of 2003, Zamzows broke ground for a new 12,000-square-foot Thrive packaging plant in Nampa. A beautifully landscaped, majestic stone-block building now occupies what once was a vacant lot in front of the Save-a-Tree manufacturing plant.

Jim Zamzow didn't create these products for the money. In fact, he said he hoped other companies would follow the Zamzows' lead. "What's the worst that could happen? Somebody else would learn how to do this, so we made the world a better place?" Making the world a better place is what Zamzows is all about.

The Harrison Tree

The Harrison Tree story played out on the grounds of the Idaho State Capitol Building, where the 100-year-old water oak tree *(Quercus nigra)* had been planted by President Benjamin Harrison. In the early 1990s the tree had been "topped," a process that involves cutting the top off the canopy of a tree. When that happens, the tree often dies.

THAT REMINDS ME OF A STORY

The Harrison tree outside the Idaho Capitol Building

A GOOD STEWARD TO THE COMMUNITY EARTH

When Jim Zamzow read in the local newspaper the tree was going to be cut down and the only question was what to do with the wood, he knew he had to act. After discussing the tree on the Zamzows Garden Show on KBOI radio, Jim and co-host Debbie Cook drove by and looked at the tree. It didn't look that sick to them.

They checked with capitol grounds staff and found out some disturbing things. The tree and the entire capitol grounds were being watered with geothermal water. Jim immediately formed an independent task force of area tree experts. At first, the Capitol Commission resisted. They'd already made up their mind. The tree had to go. So Jim wrote them a three-page letter challenging what they'd told him.

Jim then did some *extensive* testing of the capitol's irrigation system and discovered a high level of sodium in the geothermal water. This salt water was poisoning the soil and slowly killing all of the trees and other plants on the capitol grounds. After extensive media coverage of the tree's plight and Jim's three-page letter, the Capitol Commission finally agreed to let Jim and the task force come up with a plan to save the tree.

Jim, along with Chris and Randy, the owners of C.R. Care for Trees, the Capitol's contracted tree care firm, treated the Harrison Tree with Save-a-Tree. Jim also purchased an expensive tree fractionator that pumped air, water, and nutrients into the compacted soil around the tree. Jim didn't know if the treatments would work, but it was worth a shot. After all, it's not every day you find a 100-year-old tree planted by a U.S. president.

The efforts of Jim's team worked. In a letter to Jim the following year, Roy Eiguren, president of the Idaho Capitol Commission, thanked Jim and said the Harrison Tree had new growth on it and once again was producing acorns, something it had not done for several years. The Harrison Tree didn't get sick overnight and would not get well overnight. Topping a tree is a serious matter and it may take many years for the tree to look normal again. Jim Zamzow helped save the Harrison Tree not only because he had skill and knowledge to do so, but because it was the right thing to do. More importantly, as Jim told reporter John Miller in a KTVB News story, the Harrison Tree was important to our community. This tree was important to the people of Idaho. It was part of our heritage.

Whether someone else would have stepped up to the plate and taken on the Capitol Commission to stop the Harrison Tree from being cut down, we'll never know. But Jim Zamzow stepped up and put his expertise and money where his mouth was.

Eventually the capitol went through a complete remodel. Several presidents had planted trees on the grounds that were removed during that remodel, including the Harrison Tree.

A man who used to work with the parks department called Jim one day and asked him to go out for a cup of coffee. The man made pencils, and he gave Jim a beautiful pen holder with a pencil in it. The pencil was made from the Harrison oak tree.

Building Community

The west Boise rural community could always count on Carmalita Zamzow to solicit for donations. She regularly volunteered to help the American Cancer Society, the Red Cross, and Community Chest. During World War II, she helped sell war bonds and also raised money for the Red Cross to help the troops. She walked both sides of Fairview soliciting, from the County Hospital at Curtis to Cole School at Cole Road. In those days, Fairview Avenue was mostly homes. But there were a few businesses she remembers, such as the old Ragsdale Store on Fry. There were also several tourist parks like the Green Gables Motel, where people could stay overnight, and the old county hospital at Curtis.

Carmalita was humble about her volunteer work, though she worried folks might not like her doing it. She said, "It got so they'd slam the door right in my face. The poor people, I felt sorry for them, to have to answer the door and see me there begging again." But Carmalita said she continued to do the work because nobody else would do it.

A GOOD STEWARD TO THE COMMUNITY EARTH

The Zamzows do things that need to be done when no one else wants to step up. The Zamzow family and Zamzows Inc. have made a difference in the community since they came to Boise. We all can help make our community a better place by simply doing something that needs to be done.

When Jim saw the ad in the Honolulu newspaper for the very first Weed Eater, he also saw an ad for the Honolulu Humane Society. It showed a picture of a very sad, homeless puppy with the headline *"Please Adopt Me.* Paid for by Smith's Pet Shop, Honolulu. We proudly support the Honolulu Humane Society." This ad really made an impression on Jim. When he returned to Boise, he and Rick began to run similar ads in the *Idaho Statesman* showing a picture of a sad dog with the headline: *"Please Adopt Me.* Paid for by Zamzows, 6313 Fairview Ave., Boise. We proudly support the Idaho Humane Society."

Needless to say, those ads really helped get the word out about the Idaho Humane Society, then very small and new. The ads also helped bring attention to Zamzows in a positive way. Rick Zamzow did a lot of early work to support the Idaho Humane Society. When the Idaho Humane Society needed help with anything, Zamzows was there.

Zamzows sponsors two other fundraisers for The Idaho Humane Society. Zamzows Frisbee Fest was started in August of 1993 as a fun event for dogs who like to catch frisbees, with free admission for spectators. The money raised from the sale of concessions goes to the Idaho Humane Society, who supplies the volunteers who staff this fast-paced event. Frisbee Fest takes place at Ann Morrison Park in the third week of September. There are usually close to 100 dogs that compete for prizes supplied by Zamzows, and hundreds of spectators show up with blankets and lawn chairs to watch the dogs race down the 200-foot field to catch the frisbee. Judges for the event have varied over the past 28 years with one exception: Dee Fugit, the longtime Education Director of the Idaho Humane Society, started as a judge in 1993 and has returned every year through 2019. In fact, Zamzows Frisbee Fest has taken place every year, rain or shine, since 1993—except for 2020 when all public events at Ann Morrison Park were canceled due to the COVID-19 pandemic. It is hoped that Zamzows

THAT REMINDS ME OF A STORY

Frisbee Fest can resume in 2021, and that Dee Fugit will once again join them as their head judge for this fun and exciting event.

The second event that Zamzows helped start in 1993 was See Spot Walk, which was organized by Dee Fugit of the Idaho Humane Society. Having just put on the very successful Frisbee Fest that August, Zamzows was asked to help organize and promote the very first dog walk to benefit the Idaho Humane Society. Art Gregory, Zamzows' new communications and marketing director, worked with Dee in planning the initial See Spot Walk, which was held at Fort Boise Park. Zamzows ran radio ads inviting the public to participate and helped supply prizes for the winning dogs and dog-walkers. Later, a variety of contests were added to the event, and Zamzows supplied the prizes for them too.

Initially, there were only four sponsors for the first See Spot Walk, and Zamzows is the only remaining sponsor who is still in business. Each year, See Spot Walk has grown, and it is now the largest yearly fundraiser for the Idaho Humane Society, with over 3,000 dogs participating.

That first year, only 300 dogs participated in the walk, which wound its way up Mountain Cove Road and then circled back to Fort Boise Park. Mayor Brent Coles started off the walk by urging the dogs on with a megaphone. There were prizes and treats for the dogs when they returned. Today that same format is still followed, but the walk has been moved to the Julia Davis Bandshell and now takes place on paved city streets, which are blocked off from traffic during the walk. Zamzows always has a booth there, where they give out free Zamzows dog treats and samples of Zamzows and Grandma Z's dog food. Zamzows also runs radio ads promoting the event and participants can pre-register for the walk at any Zamzows store.

During the pandemic of 2020, See Spot Walk became a virtual event but was still tremendously successful. Zamzows stepped up promotion at their 13 stores by outfitting all of their employees in custom T-shirts that advertised the popular event. The result was a record number of in-store registrations, with one sales associate at Zamzows' State Street store selling over $2,000 in registrations. Zamzows is committed to helping the community no matter what obstacles are presented. And just like Frisbee Fest, the company's goal is fun for the pets and the people who love them.

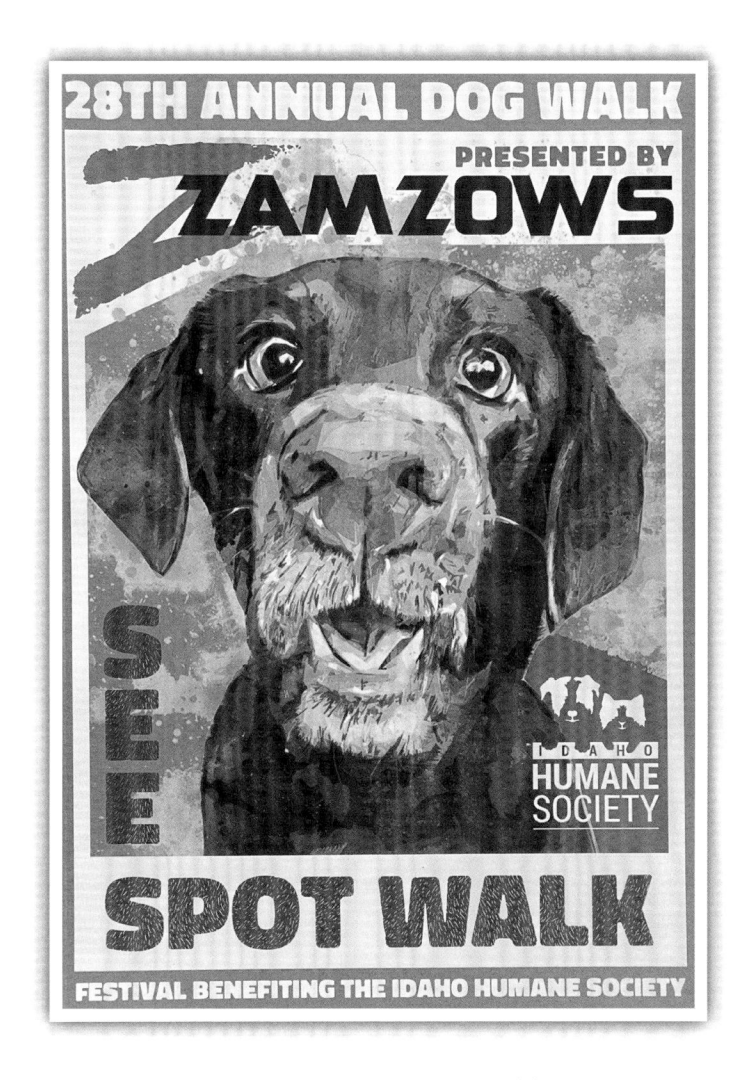

See Spot Walk charity event sponsored by Zamzows

Each Christmas season for 35 years, Zamzows helps homeless pets in the community with their Santa Paws fundraiser, where Idaho Humane Society and Boise Southwest Rotary Club volunteers dress up in a giant dog costume with a Santa Claus suit. Pets of all types show up at Zamzows stores to have their pictures taken on Santa Paws' lap. The modest fee for the picture goes to the Idaho Humane Society in Boise or Pet Haven in Nampa and is used to spay and neuter homeless pets. Zamzows pays all the expenses for the event and runs extensive radio advertising to promote it, allowing the two charities to keep 100 percent of the proceeds. Customers love bringing their animals to Zamzows and getting an annual photo of them and their pets, and in fact, many have been doing so for years, making Santa Paws a family tradition and the Treasure Valley's longest running fundraiser for pets.

Zamzows' contributions to the community go well beyond animal rescue charity. Zamzows has sold fresh-cut Christmas trees since the 1930s during the Great Depression. In fact, Grandma Z says Zamzows started the first Christmas tree lot in Boise.

At that time, everybody would cut their own Christmas trees because there wasn't enough money to buy them. Just before dark, a poor fellow came into the store looking very cold with a bunch of trees to sell. Zamzows took the whole load of trees and charged only 25 cents apiece. Grandma Z said, "Those trees just flew out of there. We sold every one we had! After that, we sold Christmas trees every year, and I think it must have been the first Christmas tree lot in Boise."

These days, Zamzows buyers travel to Oregon and hand-pick the trees, choosing the biggest and best-looking trees they can find. Then in late November, they are fresh-cut and rushed to Boise via truck that same day, often in several shipments. In 2020, Zamzows sold every tree they had. However, in past years, depending on the economy and the availability of trees, Zamzows sometimes had a few trees left. So in 2011 and 2012, and as recently as 2019, Zamzows decided to offer all of their remaining trees, regardless of size or price, for a donation in any amount to a local charity.

In 2011, Zamzows donated over $2,000 from Christmas tree sales to the Wyakin Warrior Foundation, and about that same amount in 2012 to the Boise Rescue Mission's Veterans Transitional Living Program. In 2019, Simply Cats, Boise's no-kill feline adoption center, was the selected charity. In all cases, 100 percent of the money Zamzows took in from the remaining trees was donated to charity. Zamzows even paid for radio ads to tell the public they could get a top-quality Christmas tree for whatever they wished to donate.

One memorable story took place at the Nampa store, located across from Karcher Mall. A young mother came into the store asking if it was true that she could get any tree for whatever amount she could donate. The store manager told her yes, any tree. The lady then explained that her husband was out of work and they had a home with a very tall living room and needed the tallest tree she could get. The manager found her a tree that was over 10 feet tall and had a retail price of over $200.

The woman asked sheepishly, "How much for that tree?"

The manager said, "Whatever you can donate."

The lady pulled out her purse and found $1.86 in loose change.

The manager said, "That will work."

Much to the lady's astonishment, he began to carry the tree over to her minivan parked next to the lot. Her two school-age children were inside watching, and when that huge tree began to approach their van, they began jumping up and down with joy, knowing that they were going to have a tree this Christmas and it was not going to look like Charlie Brown's. The woman was crying tears of joy when she left. Zamzows cleared all of their lots, and some worthwhile charities received checks from Zamzows. It was a great way to make everyone happy, and Zamzows was very pleased to do it.

The story of the 500 dogs in Fruitland is even more amazing. An elderly eastern Oregon woman and her husband were keeping over 500 dogs in their rural home near Ontario. When local authorities first went to the couple's home on January 22, 2003, they found dogs living in conditions beyond anything they'd ever seen. Feces were everywhere, not to mention the sight of the starving, sick, and neglected dogs.

The rescue began immediately. Hundreds of the dogs were taken to the nearby Second Chance Animal Shelter. Hundreds more went to the Idaho Humane Society in Boise and to other nearby animal shelters. Sadly, some dogs were so far gone they had to be put down. The news covered the story extensively. Zamzows had already responded by donating 1,000 pounds of Zamzows Dog Food to the cause. At the suggestion of the Fairview store manager Jim Martin, Zamzows started a donation collection at all of their stores.

THAT REMINDS ME OF A STORY

Zamzow company officials were in constant contact with the Idaho Humane Society, who had helped coordinate the rescue efforts. On Friday afternoon, a Boise Hewlett-Packard employee started a collection at H.P. She needed someone she could trust to collect and keep the money, plus a convenient location for weekend donations. She called Zamzows, who agreed, offering to account for all donations and ensure they went to the proper place.

By Monday afternoon, just three days after the first announcement of the rescue effort, Hewlett-Packard employees had donated over $1,800. Zamzows customers donated an additional $8,000, and hundreds of others brought in blankets and towels for the dogs, along with other needed items.

By 3 p.m. on Monday, Zamzows had a semi-truck loaded with 16 pallets of supplies and pet food. By 4 p.m., the truck was on its way to Fruitland. Traveling with the truck was the Zamzows president and brand manager, who carried checks and cash totaling over $10,000. When the Zamzows truck arrived, the director of the Second Chance Animal Shelter in Fruitland began to cry. The outpouring of love and compassion from the community was more than she could deal with.

Zamzows continued their collection efforts and sent several more substantial contributions to the Fruitland Shelter and to other area shelters that had been hit hard trying to deal with all the dogs they had to feed and place in new homes. Three weeks later, Zamzows ran paid radio ads featuring the Idaho Humane Society's shelter manager Pat Vance and Rick Zamzow. Pat and Rick thanked the public for their generous outpouring of love and reported that virtually all of the rescued dogs had been adopted or sent to shelters where they soon would be adopted. It was over. The instant public response to the plight of these dogs reminds us of what a community can do when they work together to accomplish something that needs to be done.

It's clear that Zamzows' heart is in the community. While they've done many charitable things, none of it has been for profit. People know if you're sincere or not when you do a good deed, whether you're subtle about it or whether you're outright. They can tell the difference. Make a genuine effort to bring good to your community, because being good to the community pays off in the long run.

A GOOD STEWARD TO THE COMMUNITY EARTH

Community Is Important

Zamzows Inc. has contributed greatly to building better communities. For example, in 1995, Zamzows helped raise the necessary funds to build a new state-of-the-art animal shelter for the Idaho Humane Society and donated another $50,000 to the Idaho Humane Society to create the Zamzows Education Room. That new Shelter served the Humane Society well for 25 years but was eventually outgrown and has been replaced by a new shelter located on Bird Street just off Overland Road in Boise. The Zamzows Education room now serves as an intake facility for animals entering the shelter.

Jim and Faye Zamzow have taken a personal interest in animal welfare and have nursed abused and neglected horses back to health when the animal shelter could not care for them. Zamzows also helped pass a bond election to build the new Canyon County Animal Shelter.

Beyond just animals, Zamzows also supports Boise State Public Radio and Idaho Public Television by airing underwriting announcements and participating in their annual pledge drives. Jim has his own helicopter and donates his time and aircraft to the Ada County Sheriff's Office to help locate lost people and capture escaped criminals. To be able to do this, Jim put himself through the Sheriff's rigorous deputy-training program and became an Ada County Sheriff's Reserve Deputy. He volunteers his services to help the community.

Kids and schools are part of our community too and many have benefited from Zamzows' community-building efforts. In 2001, Zamzows and the Tetra company donated a free 20-gallon aquarium setup to *every* elementary school in the Boise, Meridian, and Nampa school districts, a $12,000 contribution. The program, called Aquademics, was designed to help teachers show students how life, water, and ecosystems all work together in a delicate balance. Zamzows has donated plants, soil, and pots to various area elementary schools to help teach kids how seeds grow into plants and as a way to thank teachers for their dedication.

In April 2003, the Roxanne Zamzow Memorial Field was dedicated. The five youth soccer fields are located on land owned by the Friendship Celebration

THAT REMINDS ME OF A STORY

Church on Chinden Boulevard between Locust Grove and Meridian Roads. Roxanne Zamzow was Rick Zamzow's high school sweetheart and they were married for 30 years. She volunteered her time to coach girls' youth soccer and took her team, the Les Bois United, to the semi-finals. She passed away in April of 2002 of a rare heart ailment, but with the creation of Roxanne Zamzow Memorial Field, she will never be forgotten.

Roxanne and Carmalita at her 104th birthday celebration

In 2019, Jim and Rick Zamzow worked with the City of Kuna to convey 17 acres of land for a new city park. The land, which is located south of Kuna along West Shoreline Street, had been owned by the Zamzow family for many years and had appreciated immensely in value. But rather than sell it outright and take the profits to the bank, the Zamzow family answered a higher call, the need for a large city park in the growing community of Kuna. As part of the agreement, Zamzows conveyed the land to the city as a donation. The new park will be named Helen Zamzow Park and will include large, open grass areas that can be used for soccer and football fields, and perhaps softball as well. Withrow said in a September 25, 2019, interview that the city gets so many requests for soccer and football fields, and they don't have the facilities. This gesture by the Zamzow family will improve the quality of life for the residents of Kuna for many years to come. Thus, the name Helen Zamzow will live on forever and be synonymous with families spending time together and enjoying the great outdoors, which is what Zamzows is all about.

The cast of CATS at Zamzows for fundraiser

Also in 2019, Zamzows sponsored the award-winning musical *Cats* at the Nampa Civic Center. Music Theatre of Idaho produced the show and needed help paying for the set and other production elements. Zamzows helped with a cash donation and even helped move the sets from the practice hall to the Civic Center. Then Zamzows promoted the show in a number of fun and unique ways. Zamzows' co-CEOs Callie and Jos Zamzow (Jim Zamzow's daughter and son) met with the director of Simply Cats, the Boise-based cageless, no-kill feline adoption center. Working with Idaho Music Theatre, Zamzows donated 100 tickets to the musical *Cats* to Simply Cats. The shelter then resold the tickets to the public, with Simply Cats keeping 100 percent of the proceeds.

In addition to the ticket sales, Jos and Callie arranged for a different *Cats* cast member to do a live appearance at all 13 Zamzows stores. They called the

Saturday event "Cat-er-day." The public was invited via paid radio ads to come to any Zamzows store and have their picture taken with different cast members, who were there in full-costume, dressed like cats. Finally, at each night's show, Simply Cats set up an information table in the lobby of the Nampa Civic Center with a donation box, where they collected hundreds of dollars in donations from happy theater-goers. Overall, it was a huge success for everyone involved, especially Simply Cats and Music Theatre of Idaho. You might say it was the cat's meow.

All of these examples show how members of the Zamzow family and Zamzows Inc. have worked to build a better community, both on a local level and the community of the earth itself. By doing the right thing for the land, they support the community of the earth, which we are all a part of. We are all stewards of the communities in which we live, work, and play. Let's work together to build them, sustain them, and make them better.

Conclusion

These stories teach more than just the good business principles outlined in the Zamzows Ten Commandments. They teach the basic concepts of life, things like being honest, doing what's best for another person, and doing a little more than you have to do. Most things in life involve hard work and while you may think you can take a shortcut, you usually end up having to backtrack and go the correct route to get where you want to go in life.

Zamzows has insisted on quality standards since 1933. Someone else may be a good model for you in life or business, but ultimately you have to live your own life or develop your own business. You can't simply try to copy theirs.

If you are creative and develop methods in life and business that work for you, they are yours if you have the courage to see them through. That may take time, because the good things in life and business are worth working for, waiting for, and protecting once you earn them. Earning them over the long haul is usually the only way you get them and the best way to appreciate them.

You can learn a lot from others in life and business. And when seeking friends or employees, if you pick good ones and treat them right, they'll stick around.

Money can get you in a lot of trouble if you spend more than you make. And if you ever have to borrow money, pay it back quickly. You never know when you may need to borrow again.

Taking on more than you are capable of handling can get you into serious trouble. Bigger and better have different meanings. Better usually wins out, so concentrate on that and forget about being bigger. Size is a matter of function. Things work best when they are the size they need to be.

THAT REMINDS ME OF A STORY

Lastly, the earth is one big community. It may be made up of a lot of smaller communities, but we all share the same planet. It's in our own best interests to take care of our planet and preserve its resources. Grandma Zamzow understood that we can't just take things out of the earth without putting as much, or even a little more, back. The same applies to life in general and to our communities.

These values are part of what has kept the Zamzows company running since 1933, and the stories keep them from being forgotten. The Zamzow family and Zamzows Inc. uphold these values and set an example for their community, encouraging others to do the right thing for their families, neighbors, animals, and the earth.

The Bernie Zamzow family with Karen, Jim, Rick, and the seven grandchildren

Zamzows Now

Left to right: Faye Zamzow (owner), Clint Scott (son-in-law), Josua Zamzow (co-CEO), Deana Zamzow (daughter-in-law), Jim Zamzow (owner), and Callie Kaye Zamzow (co-CEO)

Siblings Callie Zamzow and Josua Zamzow, current co-CEOs of Zamzows Inc.

THAT REMINDS ME OF A STORY

Fairview store in 2021

The Zamzows store on Overland Road

Zamzows Chinden Boulevard store

ZAMZOWS NOW

ZamZoo at the Overland store selling small pets and fish

153

THAT REMINDS ME OF A STORY

An original Zamzows delivery truck sits in front of the Chinden Store

A variety of indoor house and pond plants inside Zamzows store

The Chinden store's greenhouse, which is the largest in Idaho

Acknowledgments

Art Gregory

This book represents the end of a long journey that started in 1998 when I returned to college at Boise State University. Five professors introduced me to the power of storytelling and how communication is really "the creation of community." Dr. Peter Lutze, Dr. Marvin Cox, and my Graduate Committee consisting of Dr. Ben Parker, Dr. Mary Rohlfing, and Dr. Ed McLuskie provided me with the academic foundation I needed to see that Zamzows Inc. was a living example of how stories can create and sustain company culture. I use what I learned at Boise State every day in my job at Zamzows and wish to gratefully acknowledge these five professors, as well as the dozens of others I had the opportunity to learn from.

Bringing this book from the shelves of Albertsons Library to the shelves of local book stores, retail outlets like Zamzows, and online sellers has been a monumental task. The staff of Aloha Publishing, led by Maryanna Young, has been remarkable. Photo specialist Heather Goetter and lead editor Megan Terry have been wonderful to work with and provided valuable guidance throughout the long process.

But the real heroes of this book are the members of the Zamzow family, especially Jim Zamzow. It is they who have committed these valuable stories to memory and taken the time to tell them to others. I have heard many of the stories in this book multiple times during the 29 years I have worked for Zamzows. In fact, Jim still tells the story of the first radio ads I wrote and produced for Zamzows way back in 1974! I was 21 years old and Jim was 26.

Almost 50 years later, Jim and I are still great friends, and I am still writing and producing ads for Zamzows. There's nothing I'd rather do than taking an idea and turning into a written script that comes to life on the airwaves and "moves the needle" selling the high quality lawn, garden, feed, and pet supplies that Zamzows proudly offers.

So to the members of the Zamzow family, thank you for allowing me, an outsider, to capture these verbal stories and preserve them in printed form. I also wish to gratefully acknowledge my friend and boss Jim Zamzow for his steadfast commitment to publish this book, and for working with me to make it happen.

Finally, along with my own family, I'd like to thank my "second family," Jos and Callie Zamzow, the senior management of Zamzows, and the entire staff of Zamzows who have treated me like family for the past 29 years. Thank you, and here's to many more years of success and growth at Zamzows Inc. I have to close now—it's time to record radio ads.

Jim Zamzow

First I'd like to thank Art Gregory for having the foresight and interest to record these stories and for our lifelong friendship.

Thank you to all those family members and employees whose picture appear in the book.

And thanks to my brother, Rick; my father, Bernard; and my Grandma, Carmalita Zamzow, whose stories, along with my own, make up the book.

Thank you to my wife, Faye Zamzow, for believing in this book from the start, for her help in editing, and for her patience in the process.

About the Authors

Art Gregory

Born in Ontario, Oregon, Art grew up watching television and discovered a passion for commercials and jingles. In 1957, Art's family moved to Boise, where he grew up and attended Boise schools and Boise State College. During his high school and college years, Art worked as an announcer at several local radio stations, including KBOI, and eventually became the program director of KYME Radio. It was in this role that Art first met Jim Zamzow, who had just become the manager of the Fairview store.

In 1974, Art produced and voiced a series of ads for Zamzows' dog food and continued to write and voice ads for Zamzows while working in radio until the 90s. In 1990, Art persuaded Jim to start voicing Zamzows radio ads himself. Two years later, Art became the director of corporate communications and marketing for Zamzows and formed an in-house advertising agency and recording studio. While working full time at Zamzows, Art returned to Boise State University and earned his master's degree in communications in 2003. His master's thesis, "How Zamzows Defines Its Organizational Culture Through Storytelling," is the basis for this book.

Art was an adjunct professor of communications at Boise State University for 13 years and still works full time writing and producing ads for Zamzows. He's been married to his wife, Patty, for 38 years. He is the proud father of three children—Jeremy, Michael, and Isabella—and has five grandchildren—Teija, Amaya, Demitri, Ava, and Adelina. He is the founder and president of the History of Idaho Broadcasting Foundation, a nonprofit charity with members spanning the entire nation.

THAT REMINDS ME OF A STORY

Jim and Art recording Zamzows radio advertisements

ABOUT THE AUTHORS

Jim Zamzow

Jim is the eldest grandson of the founders of Zamzows Inc. and grew up working in the family business. He attended Boise State College the year it became a four-year-school, graduating with an associate's degree in business.

He joined the Idaho Air National Guard during the Vietnam War, and when he returned, he managed a pizza restaurant and retail store before becoming the manager of the newly rebuilt Fairview Zamzows store in the early 1970s. He and his brother, Rick, expanded the company's focus from fuel and animal feed to a lawn, garden, and pet superstore, which now operates 13 stores in the Treasure Valley.

In 1990, Jim became the media spokesman for Zamzows on radio and television commercials and has become a household name in the Treasure Valley. Jim is a licensed airplane and helicopter pilot and a fifth-degree black belt Renshi in the international school of Karate Doshinkan. He's a devoted husband to his wife, Faye, and a loving father to his two children, Jos and Callie, who are now co-CEOs of Zamzows Inc. He has five grandchildren—August, Claire, Adeline, Rafielle, and Charlie.